127115

— ובא השמש —
SUNSET

SUNSET

Stories of Our
Contemporary Torah Luminaries *zt"l*
and Their Spiritual Heroism

by
HANOCH TELLER

in collaboration with
Marsi Tabak

New York City Publishing Company

To the memory of those "Gedolim"
whose voices we were too deaf to hear
and whose examples we were too indolent to follow

Rabbi CHAIM P. SCHEINBERG

KIRYAT MATTERSDORF
PANIM MEIROT 2
JERUSALEM, ISRAEL

הרב חיים פנחס שיינברג

ראש ישיבת "תורה אור"
ומורה הוראה דקרית מטרסדורף
ירושלים טל.819122

מכתב תהילה

ב' מר חשון חשמ"ז

כבר מפורסם בין דוברי אנגלית הכשרונות של
הר"ר חנוך יונתן טלר שליט"א לתאר מאורעות ולספר
סיפורי תולדות גדולי עמנו. מאד שמחתי שהר"ר
חנוך יונתן שליט"א לקח על עצמו לכתוב את תולדות
חתני האהוב והיקר הגאון רבי ניסן אלפערט זצ"ל
שנקטף בעבו וצמידת ינ יקתו מחורת רבו מרן
הרשכבה"ג רבי משה פיינשטיין זצוק"ל.

ללא ספק תולדות הגה"ר ניסן אלפערט זצ"ל
יכולים לחנך את בני עמנו להתפעל ממעשיו הכבירים
ומלימודו בתורת ה' הבלתי פוסקת. גם השכיל
המחבר בכחיבתו הנעימה לתאר גודל רוממות ערכו של
מורנו הגאון ר' משה פיינשטיין זצ"ל ויחסו
המיוחד לתלמידו המובהק והחביב הגאון רבי ניסן
זצ"ל.

כידוע החזון איש זצ"ל מאד שבח את לימוד
תולדות גדולי ישראל, ובודאי פרי עט המחבר הוא
ע יום מהודר של כוונת מרן זצ"ל. ובהיות שאני
מכיר את גודל הביקוש בין דוברי אנגלית לספרים
המושכים את הלב, הכחובים על טהרת הקודש, לכן
אני מברכו שיפוצו מעיונותיו חוצה, ויהא ספר זה
נדבך נוסף בעבודתו בשטח הזה.

יפה עשה הרב המחבר שליט"א שהוא מצרף
לקונטרס החשוב הזה את חולדותיהם של רובם של
גדולי ישראל שנפטרו בעשור האחרון. חבל על
דאבדין ולא משחכחין ומקצח נחמה יש לנו בספר הזה
שמעלה את זכרונם ומעורר הקוראים ללכת בדרכיהם
הנשגבים.

והנני מברכו שיצליח בכל מעשה ידיו לרומם
קרן החורה והיראה, ומי יחן שנזכה לראות הליכה
בדרכיהם הקדושים ויחמלא החלל הגדול שנוצר
בהסחלקותם, ונזכה לראות בביאת גואל צדק במהרה
בימנו אמן.

חיים פינחס שיינברג

בית מדרש גבוה דאמריקה בא"י
BETH MEDRASH GOVOHA OF AMERICA IN E. ISRAEL

Rabbi Aharon Kotler Institute for Advanced Learning   בית מדרשו של רבנו הגדול מרן הגאון ר' אהרן קוטלר זצוקללה"ח

Rabbi Yaakov E. Schwartzman *Dean*	הרב יעקב א. שורצמן ראש הישיבה
Rabbi Shlomo Wolbe *Principal*	הרב שלמה וולבא מנהל רוחני

לכבוד ידי"ן מעלת הרב מעלת כ"ר יחי' שלום וברכו'!

...

Contents

ב"ה

Preface

I
N MY TEACHING and in my writing, I have always employed the short story as a vehicle of instruction. A story's capacity to fascinate audiences and capture their attention endows it with the power to convey a message or impart a lesson which, it is hoped, will be remembered long after the details of the story itself are forgotten.

The stories of our contemporary *Gedolim* are the most powerful vehicles of all, for they are stories of mortal men who walked the same streets we walk, breathed the same air we breathe, ate the same foods we eat... and yet our achievements fade to shameful nothingness alongside theirs. Only by studying their lives and following in their footsteps can we hope to reach the lowest rung of the ladder they climbed. If in addition we absorb and assimilate their great lessons, then only the Almighty knows to what soaring heights we might be privileged to ascend.

The Sages declare: "*Tzaddikim bemissasam kru'im chayim,*" the saintly *Gedolim* who have been summoned to the Heavenly Assembly live on! The aim of *Sunset* is to reflect the eternal truth of *Chazal*'s statement. Reb Chaim Shmuelevitz, the Steipler Gaon, Reb Yaakov Kamenetzky,

Reb Moshe Feinstein live on in our hearts and minds. By proclaiming their message for all to hear, and emulating their piety for all to see, we demonstrate their continuing contribution to our generation and all generations to come. Thus they live on in our bodies and in our souls.

There are, regrettably, several conspicuous ommissions from this collection of *Roshei Yeshiva* and chassidic Rebbes who passed away in this decade, among them one who has had a profound effect on me personally. They too marked the lives of so many — myself included — in such unique and memorable ways, that I felt, in the brief time allotted me before publication, I would be unable to do justice to their stories.

I AM INDEBTED to those who helped me write this book. The families of the *Gedolim* were most cooperative, as were their students and followers. I am gratified to have had the privilege of meeting and speaking with many of those about whom I have written; in many instances I was able to call upon my own personal recollections. (In the biographical sketches of Reb Moshe, Reb Yaakov and the Bostoner Rebbe *zt"l,* I have focused upon only one aspect of their multifaceted, illustrious personalities.)

The Almighty has continued to shower me with blessings. With His help, I have managed to publish five books in less than three years. I pray He will endow the present volume with as much success as its predecessors have enjoyed.

My wise and talented collaborator, MARSI TABAK, has graciously allowed me once again to benefit from unmatched expertise. As ever, the dedicated assistance offered contributed significantly to the expeditious completion of this work.

Thanks are also due Rabbi Joseph Goldberg for patiently reviewing the galleys. His cogent suggestions and comments were most helpful.

I extend my gratitude to the publishers of *Good Fortune* magazine for allowing me to reprint my piece on the Steipler which appeared recently in their pages.

I thank my dear parents who I hope will derive some *nachas* from this book or at least view it as vindication of my claim that "I am busy with a project," an excuse which foiled many of their attempts to reach me.

It is customary for authors to list their children in their preface and thank them for their assistance. Thank God, the number of our children has been steadily growing, and I feel in this instance it would be more appropriate for me to apologize to them for the attention I have denied them because of my work.

It is due only to the supreme valor and remarkable forbearance of my helpmate that I am able to accomplish so much. "Her children rise and bless her; and her husband praises her." May the Almighty grant us both the privilege of seeing our children and children's children continue to follow the examples and ideals set forth in these pages.

קטונתי מלתאר זיו דיוקן מאורות הדור. ברם אין אני בן־חורין
לפטור עצמי. וכבר אמרו ז״ל, ״הוה מתאבק בעפר רגליהם.״
אפרוש כפי למרום, לבל אכשל בקולמוסי, ולא אכשל בעטי.
ילָמדו מכאן אורחות חיים ויתעלה שמיה דקודשא בריך הוא.

Hanoch Teller
Jerusalem תו״י
Tu B'Shvat 5747 / February 1987

Introduction

 "**K**LAL YISRAEL,**"** remarked the Chazon Ish, *zt"l*, "acts as an acid test in identifying its *Gedolim.*" With neither election campaigns nor parliamentary procedures, we have always been able to perceive and determine our outstanding scholars and pious leaders.

And it is this very ability, this intuitive sense of recognition, which renders us so keenly aware of the magnitude of the losses we have suffered over the past decade. Had we not recognized their greatness, we would be more readily consoled.

The Torah relates that when Moshe *Rabbeinu* learned he was to be prohibited from entering the Holy Land, his primary concern was for the Nation's well-being. Immediately, he asked the Almighty to "appoint over the congregation a man..." — not just any man, but one possessed of these essential qualities: "[one] who may lead them out and who may bring them back, that the congregation of the Lord be not as sheep which have no shepherd" (*Bamidbar* 27).

The very same characteristics can be ascribed to our spiritual shepherds: they "lead us out," with their direction and discretion honed by the lessons they have learned from the Torah, and "bring us back," guiding us and guarding over us that we not be led astray by any current antithetical to Judaism.

One need not wait for proclamations or news conferences delineating policy directions to be followed; our leaders' very being and lifestyle speak volumes. Every action — from sleepless nights submerged in the sea of the Talmud, to profound concern for the needs of a small child — serves to instruct.

Mistaken is the individual who believes that our *Gedolim* dwell in the Ivory Tower of scholarship, removed from the doings and events of the times. Invariably, they are ahead of their times, unafraid to take daring actions and provide guidance and instruction in sensitive areas.

TWENTY YEARS AGO, a copy of the *New York Times,* folded to the editorial page, caught my eye. I was just beginning to learn to read at the time, and the bold-face title of a leader intrigued me. It read: "ACHARAI." It was not until my fifteenth attempt to unscramble the word that I was able to grasp the *Times* editor's intent.

It was June 1967, and the writer was commenting on the credo of the victorious Israeli commanders in the Six Day War. *"Acharai"* in Hebrew means "after me," and with this single word the author had eloquently highlighted the difference between Israel and her enemies. Israel's troops did not march leaderless into battle, at the behest of a faceless voice issuing orders from behind a barricade or in the relative comfort and safety of a bunker. Israeli commanders led the attack, and called on their troops to "follow me!"

Two decades have passed but the message remains with

me: a "leader" must do just that — *lead*. He must stand at the forefront and bear the brunt of the attack.

The *Gedolim* are not only erudite scholars, but courageous leaders who boldly take a stand — even an unpopular one — to defend, support and propound the dignity and sanctity of our holy Torah and its precepts. By their example, they impel us, their humble but loyal troops, to follow.

A STORY IS TOLD about the day the very first locomotive pulled into the railroad station of a tiny shtetl. The local chassidim were anxious to show this technological "miracle" to their Rebbe and witness his reaction.

The Rebbe, escorted by his followers, made his way to the depot and noted the long train of cars stretching out to beyond the horizon. Just as he was examining this modern mode of transportation, the furnace was stoked and the boiler began to heat up. Billows of black smoke belched from the chimney. The engine roared and the brakes screeched. Suddenly the wheels began to revolve, and the chugging locomotive set the entire train into motion.

"Rebbe, Rebbe," the chassidim shouted excitedly over the din, "what do you say about this incredible invention, this culmination of man's genius and resourcefulness?"

The Rebbe pondered for a moment and then replied, "I see that one fiery, hot creation can carry along with it many, many cold ones."

Every generation has had its "locomotives," but ours, we now appreciate, was especially blessed. The loss of so many of our spiritual heroes in this past decade has created a gap we fear may never be bridged. Those who have left us were the sole remnants and guardians of our treasured heritage after the *churban* of Europe.

Shlomo *Hamelech* taught: "*Vezarach hashemesh, uva hashemesh*" — before one sun sets, another is born. And we, in sorrow at the *Sunset* of this decade's Torah luminaries, anxiously wait for those new suns to shine forth.

Just Pshat
Reb Nochum Percowiz

Just Pshat

REB YAAKOV KAMENETSKY, *zt"l,* once commented that *talmidei chachamim* may be divided into two categories: those who resemble the *Chiddushei HaRim* and those who resemble the *Maharsha.*

The *Chiddushei HaRim* is a *sefer* replete with brilliant analyses, and every page manifests genius. The *Maharsha,* at first glance, is far less intellectually impressive. Upon closer inspection, however, one begins to appreciate the erudition and wisdom contained in every word.

Reb Nochum Percowiz was a *Maharsha* — a man scarcely known to the "outside world" but, among the cognoscenti of yeshiva circles, he was the quintessential *talmid chacham.* Not a public figure, Reb Nochum could only be known through his learning. And even in the realm of learning, he restricted himself exclusively to the *mesechta* which the Yeshiva was studying. The result was not only expertise, but authority. His interpretations are respected, revered — and undisputed.

FROM A TENDER AGE he worked assiduously towards this goal. When he was eleven years old, "the *illui* from Trok" (Poland) was the celebrated star at the Baranovitch Yeshiva. The *Roshei Yeshiva,* Reb Elchonen Wasserman and Reb Dovid Rappaport, took a special liking to this young student. They realized that his analytical mind and unstinting diligence would lead the youngster to greatness.

It was not easy for Reb Elchonen to part with the lad, but he had to concede that by the age of thirteen Reb Nochum was already too advanced for the Baranovitch Yeshiva.

Young Reb Nochum departed for the famed Kamenitz Yeshiva where he was to be profoundly influenced by a personality who would become his *Rebbe Muvhak:* Reb Boruch Ber Levovitz. Aside from a shared learning style, there was an element of Reb Boruch Ber's nature which found its match in his new *talmid:* humility. Reb Boruch Ber, for all of his brilliance and original thought, viewed himself as nothing more than a "disciple" of Reb Chaim Soloveitchik (Brisker). Everything which Reb Boruch Ber said or wrote had its origin, he maintained, in the words of his Rebbe. That which others perceived as his own brilliance, Reb Boruch Ber humbly asserted, was merely an ability to comprehend the words and implications of his master.

REB NOCHUM was no less self-deprecating. He remembered his Rebbe's teachings verbatim, and decades later could still recite every *shiur* he had heard with the exact intonation, emphasis and flick of the finger of the original delivery. This phenomenal capacity for "total recall" of these *shiurim* was an outgrowth of and absolutely consonant with Reb Nochum's unique personality.

Learning and life were synonymous to him; learning was his very soul. For this reason he would blissfully endure any hardship — even jeopardize his health — so as not to interfere with his learning. During World War II, when Reb Nochum was in Kobe, Japan,* he discovered that the local bread was *treif.* Since he did not know how to prepare rice, the only other available food, and finding someone who could help him do so would have entailed wasting precious time from learning, he therefore subsisted for three days... on the study of the *Rashb"a!*

Because Reb Nochum learned with *mesirus nefesh,* his learning virtually became a part of his *nefesh.* One does not forget the vital information necessary to keep on living. This axiom was true of Reb Nochum regarding not only the words of his Rebbe, but everything that he learned. Tractates and their commentaries he had not reviewed in years were as fresh in his memory as though he were currently engaged in their study.

T HE WONDERFUL RELATIONSHIP between Reb Nochum and Reb Boruch Ber came to a close when the *Rav* of Trok, Reb Aryeh Zvi Percowiz, urged his son to travel on to the Mirrer Yeshiva. Had Reb Aryeh Zvi been less of a *talmid chacham* it would have been easier to protest a move which Reb Nochum wished to avoid. But like his grandfather, the Chaishek Shlomoh, and father-in-law, Reb Nochum Greenhoiz (whom Reb Nochum was named after), Reb Aryeh Zvi was eminently qualified to render a decision in this realm.

The reluctant move to the Mirrer Yeshiva resulted in Reb Nochum's physical deliverance and salvation, because, a short time later, the Mir escaped unscathed from the advancing Nazi troops. Indeed Reb Nochum later

* One of the stations of the Mirrer Yeshiva during its escape from Nazi-occupied Europe.

commented, "I can personally attest to the fact that honoring one's father not only lengthens one's days — but can save one's life." Reb Aryeh Zvi, himself a former *talmid* of the Mirrer Yeshiva, had wished his son to benefit from the same wisdom and erudition of the scholars to which he himself had been exposed.

He escorted his fifteen-and-a-half-year-old son to the Mir and introduced him to the *Rosh Yeshiva,* Reb Eliezer Yehuda Finkel. The *Rosh Yeshiva* warmly embraced the young boy and said, "Your father is like a son to me... That makes you my grandson." It was truly a clairvoyant remark, Reb Nochum later mused, uttered by the man who was destined later to become his grandfather through marriage.

Not long after Reb Nochum's arrival at Mir, the Yeshiva commenced its tortuous trek through Russia to Japan on its way to Shanghai, China. These were trying times, and only the most diligent *masmidim,* with which the Mirrer Yeshiva was richly endowed, managed to devote their fullest concentration to their studies. Reb Nochum's application to learning at this time was not lost on the Yeshiva's *Mashgiach* and *Rosh Yeshiva.* Both Reb Yechezkel Levenstein and Reb Chaim Shmuelevitz became very attached to the new student and awarded him limitless time to discuss matters of *mussar* and *halacha.*

WHILE IN SHANGHAI, the students of the Yeshiva were allocated appointments to the American consulate for visa applications. Reb Nochum's turn fell on *Tisha b'Av,* placing him in a predicament. Achieving one's freedom to the West could not be accomplished without an interview at the Consulate. One's appearance at the appointment with the Consul was, therefore, not something to be neglected or ignored; the slightest aberration could result in the immigration request being denied. On the other hand, the laws and customs of *Tisha b'Av* also had to be taken into consideration.

Reb Nochum, unlike all the other refugees, was not overawed by the Americans. To the amazement of all, he entered the Consulate without shoes, in soiled clothing, and unshaven. Many have pointed to this incident as an indication of Reb Nochum's stalwart adherence to *halacha* — even when its observance posed personal risk. Reb Avigdor Nebanzahl highlighted another point: Reb Nochum no doubt, was pleased that it worked out this way for had his turn been on any other day, it would have inevitably entailed *bitul Torah*.

Ironically, Reb Nochum's involvement in Torah, most especially in learning *bechevrusa* with Reb Leib Mallin for the entire five years of the exile, resulted in his failure to receive his visa to America. Somehow he did manage to leave Shanghai, but his destination was Canada.

Separation from the Mirrer Yeshiva, which had arrived in the interim in America, was very painful for Reb Nochum. Far more than the camaraderie, he mourned the fact that he was missing out on learning *Meseches Kiddushin* with the Yeshiva. Many years later he still maintained that *Kiddushin* was his "weakest" *mesechta,* due to his earlier detachment from the Yeshiva.

EVENTUALLY Reb Nochum was able to enter America whereupon he immediately joined the Mirrer Yeshiva, then temporarily situated in East New York. The current *Rosh Yeshiva* of the Mir in New York, Reb Shmuel Birnbaum, became his *chevrusa* and the two scholars learned the *seder* of *Kodshim* during a daily session which began at two o'clock in the afternoon and lasted until two o'clock in the morning.

By this time the predictions of Reb Elchonen and Reb Boruch Ber had long been fulfilled: Reb Nochum had become a renowned *talmid chacham,* a distinguished *mechadaish* — and also a most eligible bachelor.

Reb Chaim Shmuelevitz, at the behest of his father-in-law, Reb Eliezer Yehuda Finkel, was dispatched to America to bring Reb Nochum to the burgeoning Mirrer Yeshiva in Jerusalem; object: matrimony. Reb Eliezer Yehuda and Reb Chaim had had their eye on Reb Nochum for a long time with this purpose in mind, but the Shmuelevitz's eldest daughter, Ettel, simply had not yet come of age.

Now a mature young woman of nineteen, Ettel was ready at last to meet her twenty-eight-year-old match. Needless to say, Reb Nochum's journey to *Eretz Yisrael* was a fruitful one and the nuptials proceeded as planned.

DIRECTLY AFTER HIS MARRIAGE, Reb Nochum began to deliver a *blatt shiur* in the Yeshiva, a *shiur* which brought its deliverer and the institution which hosted him international fame. Hundreds of *bochurim* and *avrechim* from all across the globe flocked to the Mir to hear Reb Nochum's exemplary *shiurim* — masterpieces of elucidation and conceptualization. In his humility, Reb Nochum referred to his discourses as mere *"pshat"* — the basic interpretation of text.

What was outstanding, and at the same time characteristic of these *shiurim,* was that the interpretation which Reb Nochum offered, the fruit of hours of scholarly research, seemed thoroughly simple and elementary. After hearing Reb Nochum's explanation of the *gemara* or a *Rishon,* it was practically impossible to understand it any other way. His interpretation was the sole interpretation, the true *"pshat."*

Reb Nochum achieved this unparalleled clarity by adhering to the *Rishonim,* especially Rashi. Every line of Rashi underwent meticulous scrutiny and elucidation. The result was not only an entirely new understanding of Rashi, but a commentary far more meaningful. Reb Nochum's reasoning was irrefutable and so naturally fitting to the text that its simplicity... was simply awesome. Neither during nor after *shiur* was he wont to delve into lengthy explanations or complicated calculations. Rather, through a process of methodical dissection, Reb Nochum would melt concepts down to their most essential core, stripping away any superfluous reasoning or wordage. Only the vital essence remained in his crucible, or in Reb Nochum's terminology: just the translation — "*pshat.*"

Reb Nochum's learning process is reminiscent of, and perhaps can be best compared to a project once undertaken by the *Chachmei HaKabbalah.* These erudite mystics wished to compile a commentary on the Talmud in accordance with the Zohar. They commenced their massive undertaking and were dismayed to learn, at the very outset, that they had amassed reams and reams of material, and the commentary for just the first page appeared endlessly long.

The scholars began to condense their work, but found that it was still too lengthy. So they condensed some more. Painstakingly deleting and abridging the work, they discovered to their astonishment that they were left with... Rashi!

UNDOUBTEDLY Reb Nochum's masterful command derived from his total immersion in the subject matter — to the exclusion of all else. His concept of *inyanna d'yoma* was very predictable: it was either *Bava Metziah, Yevamos,* or *Nedarim,* etc.

One Chanukkah someone came to relate a thought connected to the Chanukkah holiday, and Reb Nochum, as always, listened attentively. He offered a warm compliment but excused himself for not delving into the matter for, "I simply cannot tear myself away from *Bava Kamma*."

When the Six-Day War erupted, the *talmidim* and occupants of the Yeshiva building (which stood only meters from the Jordanian border) descended into the bomb shelter. This was to be their home for the duration of the battle for Yerushalayim. The frequent sound of shells exploding and sporadic gunfire pervaded the shelter as some students managed to concentrate on *pirkei Tehillim* while others silently contemplated the fearful situation. Reb Nochum, however, built for himself a *shtender* of bricks and resumed learning as though nothing untoward was happening — precisely as he had while crossing Siberia into Japan and throughout the war years. Marauding Arab armies were not about to dictate to Reb Nochum when he might or might not learn.

Reb Nochum often studied late at night and whenever he would sense that he was beginning to drowse, he would raise his wooden *shtender* in the air and bang it down loudly on the stone floor. Thus he roused himself, and simultaneously demonstrated his determination that nothing would stop him from learning before his appointed time.

Reb Nochum's son once saw his father glancing at a secular book, an action inconsonant with the man's zealous refusal to waste even a second from learning. Later investigation revealed that the *Rosh Yeshiva* was suffering from an excruciating toothache, and he was for once unable to concentrate on learning. To sit idle was just as difficult.

THE PRODUCT of this rare scholarship, burning diligence, and saintly personality was not only a *talmid chacham* of outstanding proportions, but far more than that. Reb Nochum, as so many have said, became the very Torah itself.

Students and colleagues alike were baffled at Reb Nochum's knowledgeability and grasp of all the facets of the Torah, when he adhered so rigidly and exclusively to study of only the *gemara* which the Yeshiva was learning. The answer is clear: Reb Nochum embodied the holy Torah; he knew Torah as one knows one's own body, "like the back of his hand."

One who had absorbed Torah into his every fiber naturally behaves in consonance with its dictates and ethics. But in this realm as well Reb Nochum excelled, at times exhibiting virtues beyond our ken.

The master *mechadaish Torah,* he emphatically denied that he had ever inferred or developed a novel concept. The common expressions, "I have a good *vort.*" or "*Ich hab a niess*" were foreign to his lips. So self abnegating was his disposition that he participated in weekly sessions with prominent *talmidei chachamim* to discuss *their* Torah thoughts.

Reb Nochum never sat along the *mizrach* wall or in any conspicuous place which might attract attention to himself, preferring anonymity and shunning acclaim both in and out of the *beis midrash.* He was once placed at the head table at a wedding, an honor which he typically declined. "My lot," he explained, "could have been like the millions of others, including my own family, who did not manage to escape the war in Europe. I have little doubt that God spared me so that I might study and teach his Torah — not that I might receive honor."

The occasion of Reb Nochum's first *shiur klalli* was marked by a majestic procession that continues to inspire. Flanked by Reb Eliezer Yehuda Finkel on one side and Reb Chaim Shmuelevitz on the other, the young *Rosh Yeshiva* was led to the front of the *beis midrash*. The sight of these three Torah giants walking arm-in-arm up the Yeshiva aisle stirred the heart of even the most impassive *Litvak*. But those who saw Reb Nochum's expression were amazed; it was neither pride nor joy which filled his visage, but a desperate urgency to flee the honor that had been thrust upon him.

HIS UNSURPASSED HUMILITY found expression in deeds never before imagined — even by saints and scholars. Those who are endowed with a generous and philanthropic nature, including the outstanding Torah leaders from all generations, have demonstrated that there is one thing with which they will not easily part: Torah novellae. Of course, whoever develops a novel Torah thought is anxious to share it with others, have it discussed, publicized — even have it printed — provided that it is attributed to him. Not Reb Nochum. He dispensed his Torah thoughts — literally gave them away — as though he were returning them to their rightful owners.

Many wished to consult Reb Nochum or to seek his opinion on the Torah thoughts they had developed. On a daily basis dozens of students approached him with questions and ideas which they wished to verify as innovative. Not only would Reb Nochum make himself available and graciously give of his time, but he would offer a very special bonus. With unrivalled solicitude and diplomacy Reb Nochum would politely comment, "I assume you mean to ask..." and proceed to ask an incisive question and offer a masterful answer, incorporating a tapestry of interpretations of both *Rishonim* and *Acharonim.*

Clearly the person who had posed the question had never thought of such a question nor would he likely have been capable of doing so. The response was equally beyond the student's ability. Nevertheless, day after day, Reb Nochum continued to implant ingenious questions and answers into the mouths of colleagues, students and callow novices. (If the question posed was actually worthy of consideration, he would insert an answer to it in his excursus.) The following incident highlights the ludicrousness of the situation, and the Rebbe's selflessness and tact. After hearing an entire, lengthy, detailed theory supposedly based on a student's query, the disciple asked innocently, "I'm sorry, what was it again that I asked?"

TOGETHER with Reb Nochum's humility was his devotion to *emmes* — truth. He bore *emmes* like an internal polygraph by which he gauged every thought he uttered. And if something deviated from his self-imposed standards and rigid definition of *emmes,* then it was never suggested. For hours Reb Nochum would retire to his porch, sometimes for entire nights, to work on a concept until he was sure that it was absolutely true. And if a doubt ever arose, Reb Nochum would either abandon the concept or rework it — anything but offer an interpretation whose veracity was suspected.

A prime example occurred during a *Motzai Shabbos chaburah* several years ago. Every *Motzai Shabbos* during the *zman,* Reb Nochum delivered a lengthy *chaburah* which in effect was the detailed groundwork for the more concise *shiur klalli* he would give the following morning.

The fulcrum of this particular *chaburah* was the

explanation of the *Rach* on the *gemara* being studied. After the *chaburah,* which always ended very late, one of the students asked what Reb Nochum considered to be a valid question on the *Rach,* thus weakening to a small degree the thrust of his interpretation. Reb Nochum had little difficulty in both explaining the *Rach* and answering the question posed, yet this chink in the armor disturbed him. In the *shiur klalli* the next morning, Reb Nochum did not even mention the *Rach,* and the subject of the *shiur* for once differed from the *chaburah.*

It was not at all uncommon for Reb Nochum to commence a *shiur* with the announcement that he wished to retract everything which he had said the previous day because of some questions that had arisen on his interpretations. Furthermore, to make sure that he did not undeservedly receive credit, Reb Nochum went out of his way to mention the source for everything he said in his *shiur.*

Every night, in preparation for the daily shiur, he would learn in his home with four of the Yeshiva's finest students. If during the morning *shiur* Reb Nochum mentioned a point which had arisen the previous evening, he unfailingly attributed it to the other participants, even when it was incontestably his own. "Someone pointed out," or "It has been raised," were the expressions he commonly used for ideas which were fundamentally his but the thought processes which had led him to their discovery might have been initiated by another.

Keenly aware of Reb Nochum's tendency never to take credit for an idea which he could not positively assert was his own, a student was once surprised to see a concept put forth by Reb Nochum that was identical to one which was printed in Reb Elchonen's *sefer, Koveitz Shiurim.* The student asked if Reb Nochum's idea was not the same as Reb Elchonen's?

Reb Nochum responded, "I remember discussing the matter," thus revealing that it had been Reb Nochum himself who suggested the idea to Reb Elchonen.

REB NOCHUM'S advice was as valued and cherished as was his expertise in learning. Even Reb Chaim Shmuelevitz sought his son-in-law's advice on all matters which concerned the Yeshiva and *Klall Yisrael*. Reb Nochum was the essence of Torah; his advice, then, was unadulterated Torah reasoning.

This reasoning, combined with Reb Nochum's boundless dedication to Torah study, was reflected in his counsel. When one student informed the *Rosh Yeshiva* that he was about to commence his search for a wife, he received the following advice: "There is a common misconception which you must avoid. Many believe that once one begins to look for a match, this search becomes one's major occupation, and because one cannot spend the entire day meeting *shadchanim* and investigating proposed mates, there is time for learning as well.

"Following the same pattern of reasoning, once one has found his intended bride, then one's major activity becomes preparing for the wedding. A hall must be rented, an apartment must be found, a caterer selected, housewares purchased, etc. And since one cannot spend the whole day in these pursuits, one also learns.

"After the marriage, one is obliged to fulfill the Torah commandment to gladden one's wife. And thus the first year of marriage is devoted to this goal. Understandably one cannot speak with one's wife all day long, and therefore there is time to engage in Torah study.

"With the arrival of the children, one is commanded to educate them. This entails taking them to *cheder,* and, when they return home, reviewing what they have learned. Naturally children are enrolled in school for a large part of the day, thus there is time to learn.

"All of this," Reb Nochum emphasized, "is a mistake! One's job is to learn Torah, period. Time will have to be found for the other activities. I can only assure you that if you genuinely engage in Torah study the way you should, then time will be found for all of the other activities you must take care of."

A LL OF THESE sterling qualities, as well as excellence in learning methodology, this great Rebbe was able to teach his hundreds of disciples. But ironically, as Reb Nochum's popularity grew his accessibility diminished. Plagued by a debilitating disease, Reb Nochum had difficulty walking and his *shiur* was eventually transferred from the dining hall (the only room large enough to accommodate all those who wished to participate) to his apartment located in the Yeshiva building. This limited the number of students who could attend the *shiur.* At noontime every day, Reb Nochum's private quarters became public domain as one hundred and twenty *bochurim* hurriedly squeezed inside to hear their master's words.

For the *Motzai Shabbos chaburah,* however, the limit was lifted. Students poured in, positioning themselves in any space available: perched on window sills, wedged between bookcases, balanced on radiators. The door to the apartment was kept open and a speaker broadcast the *shiur* to the multitudes who had gathered for this weekly Torah attraction, students not only from the Mir but from several other yeshivos as well. Some *bochurim* ingeniously managed to pick up the *shiur* on their radios (and simultaneously taperecord it) in the comfort of their dormitory rooms since the microphone frequency used to amplify the *shiur* could be received on a weak local channel.

In or out of *shiur,* Reb Nochum cared for his students, and their spiritual welfare was uppermost in his mind. One student had difficulty arising in time for *Shacharis*. Reb Nochum's displeasure was most apparent and he was not consoled by the fact that this *bochur* — an American boy enrolled in the Mir in Jerusalem — excelled in learning.

On the day that the student was to return to America, Reb Nochum found himself even more concerned about this *bochur*'s penchant for rising late — but for a reason that was uniquely characteristic of the Rebbe. What would happen, Reb Nochum thought to himself, if this *bochur* were to rise early and be ready at four-thirty in the morning for the airport limousine? A terrible accusation, God forbid, might be hurled against the boy in Heaven! He could not get up for *davening,* but to leave the Yeshiva for America he could?!

Reb Nochum was truly agonized by this dilemma and actually prayed that the student miss his flight — for his own welfare. And when this unusual wish was fulfilled, Reb Nochum was happy and cheerful the entire day.

Reb Nochum was remarkably forbearing towards his *talmidim,* and offered assistance whenever possible, but the *Rosh Yeshiva* could be equally harsh when he deemed it necessary. A student once complained that he had been studying in the Yeshiva for five years and had not noticed any progress in his learning. Quoting the *gemara Chullin* 24 that whoever does not see a blessing after five years of learning should cease, the student had suggested that perhaps the time had come for him to leave the Yeshiva. Reb Nochum was swift in his rebuttal. "When the *gemara* suggested that if after five years of learning you have not seen a blessing, it was not referring to someone who was in yeshiva for five years but to someone who LEARNED for five years!"

THE EFFECTS of Reb Nochum's horrible disease became painfully apparent. From walking with difficulty he regressed to total confinement to a wheelchair; it seemed not a muscle in his body was spared. Remarkably, Reb Nochum appeared to be oblivious to a disease which was manifest to all. He continued his researches with the same apparent diligence and stamina as before. He did not alter his grueling schedule — rising before *davening* and learning with a *chevrusa* continuously until two-thirty in the morning without respite even for an afternoon break — as long as he was physically capable of maintaining it.

Furthermore, Reb Nochum would not permit his disease to arrest his spiritual growth. Indeed he had dozens of recorded and transcribed *shiurim* from his first years as a *gemara Rebbe,* yet he refused to refer to them. It was inappropriate, he felt, to rely on the *shiurim* which he had delivered years earlier. "I am more advanced in learning now," he reasoned, "than I was then and therefore capable of greater and more thorough comprehension."

The only thing that could conquer such an iron will was the degenerative disease which he battled daily but which proved mightier than he. Like his namesake, *Nochum Ish Gam Zu,* every organ in his body was afflicted. Concerning that suffering saint, the *gemara* relates that as long as he was around, "the house could not fall." And as long as Reb Nochum lived — although his last six years were not life as we know it — there was hope and assurance that the house would not fall...

During all those torture-filled years, Reb Nochum was tenderly cared for by his loving sons, sons-in-law, and other close relatives. They gave of their time, which often meant several sleepless nights a week, in order to lessen his suffering and ease the burden of his devoted Rebbetzen. During this period Reb Nochum was frequently rushed to the hospital, each time accompanied by his devoted attendants.

The medical staff of the hospital could not help but notice the glowing countenance of their patient, and the unmatched dedication of his assistants. They quickly perceived what thousands of disciples and admirers the world over understood so well: the man who clung so tenuously to life was one of the century's greatest luminaries and his imminent demise was a tragedy that would not easily be overcome.

PRAYERS WERE SAID with fervor, and the soul so enriched by pure Torah nourishment tarried a while longer before its ultimate departure. And when that dreaded day arrived on the eighteenth of MarCheshvan 5747, the Torah world joined with the family and the Mirrer Yeshiva in mourning and immeasurable grief.

Tens of thousands arrived at the Mirrer Yeshiva to attend the final *shiur* delivered by the *Rosh Yeshiva.* Through his incisive lessons, he had taught the Yeshiva community how to learn *gemara,* Rashi, and *"pshat."* By the modest quarters he occupied in the Yeshiva building, through which hundreds passed daily, he taught how to live humbly before the Almighty. And by his silent suffering and uninterrupted Torah study, he taught how to love God even while enduring the most agonizing pain. In every yeshiva, all across the globe, these, and every one of his brilliant *shiurim,* live on.

Rebbe Talmid
Reb Moshe Feinstein and
his disciple Reb Nison Alpert

Rebbe Talmid

HE LOVED HIS FAMILY; he loved his students; he loved his yeshiva and his community. He especially loved children and frequently stopped on the street to kiss the head of a passing schoolboy or tie a toddler's wayward shoelace. His affection for and devotion to his fellow man was legendary, but there was a special place in Reb Moshe Feinstein's heart for his favorite disciple and protégé, Reb Nison Alpert.

Their relationship spanned four decades, nourished by Torah study and sustained by mutual admiration and utmost respect. So intertwined were the lives of the Gaon and his talmid that, despite the disparity in their ages, barely two months after Reb Moshe departed from this world, Reb Nison followed. And while *Yeshiva shel Maalah* is surely enriched by their presence, *Yeshiva shel Matah* is painfully impoverished.

"Look," Reb Moshe would often exhort his students, "look at my Reb Nison! There he sits hour after hour without interruption. What a *masmid,* he even immerses his bare feet in cold water to keep himself awake."

Reb Nison's diligence was indeed noteworthy. His entire

existence was dedicated to the relentless pursuit of learning and his insatiable appetite for Torah became his trademark. Never was he seen without an open *sefer* in his hands. It was as though he had, even as a youngster, a prescient awareness that his time on this earth would be all too short and that he must not waste a single precious moment of it.

WHEN REB NISON fled from Europe to America as a child, he soon found his way to the home of the man who was to become his Rebbe, Rabbi Moshe Feinstein. Even then, at the tender age of twelve, Nison's brilliance set him apart and Reb Moshe instantly recognized his potential for greatness.

Rebbetzen Feinstein regarded Nison as one of her own children, for he was always at the house learning with and observing his Rebbe. When one day Nison inadvertently spilled a bottle of ink over a volume of Reb Moshe's cherished Shulsinger *shas,* it was the Rebbetzen who swiftly came to his rescue and claimed responsibility for the act. (Reb Moshe characteristically responded, "How beautiful the *shas* looks on blue paper.")

For many years, Nison Alpert and his Rebbe were inseparable; rarely was Nison seen other than in the company of his Rebbe. When not in Reb Moshe's home, the two could be found in Reb Moshe's yeshiva, Mesivta Tiferes Yerushalayim (MTJ) or strolling along the FDR Drive on Manhattan's Lower East Side. There, on the quiet paved walkways, surrounded by lush lawns, verdant foliage and the gently rolling East River, Rebbe and talmid engaged in their favorite pastime: plumbing the depths of Torah.

Each Friday after *shiur,* when everyone would disappear from the *beis midrash,* Reb Moshe would remain behind to replace the *sefarim* on the shelves and to turn off the lights (usually climbing onto a table to do so since he was too short to reach the string). Reb Nison naturally stayed to help — a practice which continued throughout the years.

Every Shabbos the two would walk home together from shul via a circuitous route which entailed crossing several tenement courtyards — the playgrounds of many neighborhood children. As usual, Reb Moshe would stop several times along the way to button this child's sweater or retie that one's shoelace, or to break up a spat between the youngsters. He would separate the disputing parties and plant a tender kiss on each one's head, making them feel awfully ashamed for fighting — at least in his presence.

Nison dutifully followed and imitated his Rebbe's every move. Since carrying is forbidden on Shabbos, mothers of babes in arms remained indoors with their infants while keeping a watchful eye out the courtyard window for their older offspring. The two scholars' unusual behavior, which these women witnessed weekly, brought to mind the image of Moshe *Rabbeinu* and his talmid Yehoshua, and left a lasting impression on them all.

Before Pesach one year, when Nison was yet a young teenager, a Belzer chassid approached him and Reb Moshe soliciting *maos chittim*. Reb Moshe was not carrying any money at the time but assured the fellow that he would forward a donation. A few days later, the two walked all the way to the far side of Delancey Street to locate the Belzer chassid whose exact address they had mislaid. They searched and investigated but could find neither the chassid nor a clue to his whereabouts. Day after day, Rebbe and talmid made the long, fruitless pilgrimage so that Reb Moshe could honor his word.

On *erev* Pesach, as Nison was dressing for the holiday, he was startled by urgent knocking on his bedroom door. Only partly clothed, he hurriedly opened the door to find a breathless Reb Moshe. The Rebbe, taking no notice of his talmid's attire, exclaimed, "*Koom, Nison! Ich hob gefunnen di address!*"

Ebullient with joy, Reb Moshe managed to contain his excitement long enough for Nison to finish dressing, and then led him once more to the other side of Delancey.

[On the way back from delivering the *maos chittim*, although it had begun to rain, Reb Moshe chose a roundabout route home, instead of the more direct way via Henry Street. This naturally roused Nison's curiosity but Reb Moshe explained quite simply that he wished to purchase a newspaper. To the mind of a talmid who knew his Rebbe so well, the only thing which sounded more preposterous than Reb Moshe buying a newspaper, was Reb Moshe buying a newspaper on *erev* Pesach.

Much time passed before Reb Nison found the courage to question his Rebbe concerning his apparently uncharacteristic action but by then he had figured out the answer himself: the newspaper had been for the Rebbetzen and it served as his excuse for leaving the house on *erev* Pesach. Doing a favor for his Rebbetzen was far from uncharacteristic. It was one of Reb Moshe's many gestures that expressed his affection and appreciation for his wife. Unknowingly, the Rebbe set an example which was followed by countless local *baalei battim* and *bnei Torah* — to the delight of newspaper sellers and shopkeepers alike.]

ALTHOUGH virtually all his waking hours were spent at MTJ, Nison, along with his three sisters, slept at the home of his parents. One day he intercepted a letter to them from the yeshiva indicating that his enrollment would be terminated unless tuition was forwarded immediately.

[Nison's father, Reb Shebsel, hailed from the same town

as the Chafetz Chaim and was the son-in-law of the Palonka Rav, after whom Reb Nison was named. (After his father-in-law's passing, Reb Shebsel became the Palonka Rav.) He served as a *Rosh Yeshiva* in New York since the 1930s and was wealthy in Torah scholarship but by any other standard, destitute. In the 1940's Reb Shebsel contracted a most debilitating disease that confined him to a wheel chair for the rest of his life. Possibly, the delicate state of Reb Shebsel's health contributed to the warm relationship which existed between Reb Moshe and Nison: Nison looked upon Reb Moshe as a father, and Reb Moshe graciously filled this role.]

Nison was painfully aware of his family's inability to pay the tuition fee and the thought of expulsion was devastating. Without revealing the contents of the letter to his parents, Nison locked himself up in his room and cried bitterly. Rebbetzen Feinstein, upon learning what had transpired, baked a batch of cookies with which to lure the young boy out of his solitary confinement and rushed to the scene — but to no avail.

Reb Moshe then arrived and ordered Nison to come out. The boy knew he had no choice but to obey his Rebbe. Suppressing his natural instincts and profound humiliation, he emerged and Reb Moshe drew him close and said, "Come, let us return together to yeshiva. For you there is no need for tuition."

Several years later Reb Moshe's love for his talmid and respect for his scholarship led to his insistence that Reb Nison be hired to deliver a *shiur* in the yeshiva. The board of directors of the yeshiva responded that there were already too many *Rebbeim* and consequently no need to hire a new one. Reb Moshe's reaction to their refusal changed personal history. "*Es iz mein yeshiva. Ir kent alle gayn.*" "It is my yeshiva," he declared. "If you refuse to hire him, you can all leave!" And they did. From that day forward all of the financial and other administrative responsibilities of MTJ fell squarely on Reb Moshe's shoulders.

REB NISON'S CONDUCT at MTJ was something of a curiosity. In a yeshiva not commonly known (at the time) for the superiority of its students, Nison Alpert was an anomaly. He sat in the *beis midrash* studying day and night without interruption, oblivious to the absence of learning surrounding him.

The intensity of concentration he exhibited as a youngster in yeshiva was unaltered in later years when his personal responsibilities grew, as problems developed, or when he encountered any other sort of disturbance which would distract the most dedicated of students. Nison Alpert was the ultimate *"masmid"* — and his *hasmada* was so supreme as to defy all norms and lexicons.

"Masmid" is a term generally applied to a student who displays remarkable assiduousness in his studies, learning far beyond the already demanding schedule observed in yeshivos. The term is also ascribed to one who engages in no time-wasting activities but devotes himself entirely to the task of learning Torah purely for the sake of learning. Reb Nison's brand of *hasmada,* however, was in a class by itself.

Even a colicky infant could not disturb Reb Nison's amazing power of concentration and indefatigable compulsion to learn. He quickly devised a crib-rocking apparatus out of three belts connecting the crib to the rocking chair in which he sat, balancing a *sefer* in his lap and learning while the child was lulled back to peaceful slumber. In a stifling, overcrowded subway car, under the exasperating flicker of blinking lights, Reb Nison could be found squinting at the pages of the ever-present *sefer* he clutched tightly in his hands.

Adverse conditions which would make others shudder simply to contemplate did not faze him, certainly not enough to interrupt a moment of his learning. Aside from the *beis midrash* at MTJ, one quiet place he found to learn was a tiny unheated shul. Rabbi Yeshaya Siff, the Rabbi of the Young Israel of the Lower East Side, pleaded with Reb Nison to avail himself of the facilities in the main Young Israel building which was heated. Rabbi Alpert declined the offer, explaining that creature comforts were not conducive to learning. "Where it is bitter cold, I stand little chance of falling asleep."

A scholar of Reb Nison's caliber, absorbed in his studies to the exclusion of all else, is seldom expected to have much of a personality. Reb Nison was unique in this respect. He was warm and outgoing, a patient listener and an athlete of some note. In addition, he possessed a quick wit and often elicited gales of laughter from his students and colleagues with a clever turn of phrase or particular pithy remark.

The nickname by which he was known at MTJ and which he bore without embarrassment was, surprisingly, "Johnny," an allusion, perhaps, to his athletic accomplishments and an indication of his easygoing temperament. Once, his father telephoned the *beis midrash* and asked to speak to Nison Alpert, but to Reb Shebsel's astonishment, no one seemed to know who that was! How could it be, Reb Shebsel wondered, that his son, reputed to be a true *masmid* and the *Rosh Yeshiva*'s favorite, was not known to any of the students? At last someone remembered "Johnny's" real name and promptly handed over the phone to Reb Nison.

REB NISON gained enormously from his close association with Reb Moshe, observing and adopting the outstanding character traits of his mentor. But the imprint was most apparent in the realm of learning. Although the *beis midrash* in which he learned was lackluster and failed to attract scholars of renown, it was a place where he could devote his energies entirely to his purpose without distractions. As Reb Dovid Feinstein (Reb Moshe's son) put it so well: "No one ever knew how long or how late Reb Nison learned in MTJ for no one was ever present late enough to see him leave." He could easily have chosen a different *beis midrash,* one where people would have taken notice of him, and where he would have been in the company of other *talmidei chachamim* who surely would have sought his opinion. Yet he remained at MTJ, primarily because it was the closest *beis midrash* to his home, and there, like his Rebbe, he could best engage in *Torah lishma.*

The learning style of Rebbe and talmid was similar in two essential ways: first, like his Rebbe, Reb Nison sat for countless hours every day learning all by himself. With neither *chevrusa* nor study group to spur or stimulate him, he managed to learn for extraordinary stretches of time. His own drive was sufficient incentive. Second, with each subject he studied, his keen analytical mind devised new insights and interpretations, undeterred by the lack of a forum or colleague with whom to discuss his innovative ideas. It was not until close to twenty years later that he would deliver a *shiur* to older boys, but in the interim he formulated numerous intricate *chiddushim* on the most esoteric points of *shas.*

His only audience was the ream of notebooks which he filled with his *chiddushei Torah.* Only a talmid of Reb Moshe could learn and be *mechadeish* so much Torah under such conditions. Reb Moshe did so himself in Russia thirty years earlier; who but Reb Nison could have done it in America?

The example of his Rebbe was the guiding principle in

Reb Nison's life. Upon occasion he would disagree with Reb Moshe over an interpretation, but ultimately he would accept the Rebbe's *psak.* ("If not for the *Rosh Yeshiva,* I would have ruled differently," was a line he uttered often.) In conduct, however, there was never any disagreement: Reb Nison always yielded to and defended the desires of his Rebbe.

Reb Moshe was frequently criticized for his leniency in the area of endorsements for solicitors of charity, his critics claiming that many solicitors were actually undeserving. By appending his name to their credentials, the critics argued, Reb Moshe encouraged people to contribute to a possibly undeserving cause while a legitimate one went wanting.

Reb Nison was swift to come to his Rebbe's defense. He declared that Reb Moshe was not the FBI, to probe into each person's background and history. The act of requesting charity was in itself sufficient evidence of genuine need.

Reb Nison explained the expression "*chessed ve'emmes*" (kindness and truth) in a similar light. One would imagine that *emmes* should have precedence over *chessed,* and yet the expression always appears with "*chessed*" preceding. If one were to approach everything from the perspective of "truth" and thoroughly investigate until one was certain that the complete truth was revealed, one would never arrive at "kindness." This was another lesson which Reb Nison learned well from his Rebbe.

Once the Satmar Rebbe challenged Reb Nison to justify an opinion held by Reb Moshe. With his quick wit and piercingly analytical mind, Reb Nison not only managed to refute the Satmar Rebbe in vindication of Reb Moshe, but earned a thousand dollar donation from him for Peylim, to boot.

WHEN THE MIRRER YESHIVA opened in New York, Reb Nison thought he would like to learn there. His father had been a student of the Mirrer Yeshiva in Poland, and the idea of attending a branch of the yeshiva in which his father had studied evoked a feeling of nostalgia for Reb Nison. But he did not know how to break the news to Reb Moshe. Certainly, he could not simply abandon his Rebbe for a different yeshiva without first consulting with him.

Reb Nison finally mustered the courage and made what was then an exhausting trip from the "country" in Upstate New York to lower Manhattan to inform Reb Moshe of his plans. As soon as he entered the room, however, he saw that his Rebbe was terribly distraught. "Nison," Reb Moshe began, "there is a talmid here who wishes to leave the yeshiva and go to learn with Reb Aharon..." Nison knew with those words that his fate was sealed. He could never allow himself to distress his beloved Rebbe, that was certain. And so, despite the long journey he had made just to tell Reb Moshe of his plans to leave, he never mentioned the subject.

Remaining with Reb Moshe enabled Reb Nison to learn and grow with his Rebbe on a plane achieved by no other. He fulfilled Reb Chaim Shmuelevitz's classic definition of the ideal student: "One who knows not only what the Rebbe said but what the Rebbe *would* have said."

Indeed, some thirty years ago, a number of complex *shailos* were raised as a result of a serious traffic accident and these required immediate attention. The questions were brought before Reb Aharon Kotler *zt"l*, the *Gadol Hador* of that era, but because of their delicate nature, Reb Aharon felt he must first consult with Reb Moshe before deciding.

He telephoned MTJ and asked for the *Rosh Yeshiva,* but was told that Reb Moshe was not in. "Who is this?" he asked of the young man who had answered the phone. "Nison Alpert," Reb Nison replied. "Good enough," Reb Aharon reasoned. "Speaking to you is the same as speaking to Reb Moshe."

Reb Nison's mental agility was coupled with physical strength, developed and maintained on the neighborhood handball courts. His regular partner was Reb Dovid Feinstein, and the two scholars could be seen most Fridays after Reb Moshe's *shiur* engaged in a vigorous round of the fast-paced game. When Reb Dovid was unavailable, Reb Nison would take on any other challenger with the stamina for the demanding sport and the ability to carry on an intelligent discussion while the game was in progress.

Reb Nison's athletic prowess was not limited to handball. He excelled in other sports as well, notably swimming, and once actually saved Reb Aharon Soloveitchik from drowning.

It was generally believed that Reb Nison never slept, a theory which was difficult to disprove. In fact, he slept nightly, although perhaps "fell asleep" is the more appropriate term. He would climb into bed along with a heap of volumes and continue studying until the wee hours of the morning. Usually a family member who chanced to arise in the middle of the night would gently remove his eyeglasses and close the *sefer* Reb Nison held in his hand when sleep had overcome him.

IN 1953, when Reb Chaim Pinchas Scheinberg, *Mashgiach* of Chafetz Chaim Yeshiva (and later the *Rosh Yeshiva* of Torah Ohr and Rav of the Mattersdorf neighborhood in Jerusalem), sought a suitable match for his daughter Zelda, he turned to Reb Moshe for a recommendation. Normally a prestigious *shidduch* such as this would have warranted some contemplation and consideration, but Reb Moshe had no compunctions whatsoever about his choice: Nison Alpert, the foremost *talmid chacham* in his yeshiva. Although Reb Moshe would have liked for Reb Nison to become his own son-in-law, he settled for the role of *shadchan,* content in the knowledge that the match was a good one.

The Lower East Side was ecstatic over this "local" *shidduch.* It meant that the religious community would not lose its resident scholar, as might have been the case had he chosen a *kallah* from a distant region. Reb Nison's dear friend, the Kapishnitzer Rebbe, was particularly elated; he even hosted *sheva brachos* for the new couple and maintained a warm relationship throughout the years. As was hoped, after his marriage, Reb Nison entered MTJ's nascent *kollel* and a few years later began to deliver the highest *shiur* in the yeshiva, directly below that of Reb Moshe.

Reb Nison sensed, however, that this appointment might arouse the envy of others. In order to avoid dispute and avert generating ill feelings, Reb Nison quickly relinquished the honor in favor of delivering the *shiur* for sixth- and, later, for eighth-graders. Only a man of Reb Nison's humility and patience could have accepted this lowly post, a position which neither reflected his stature nor provided much gratification.

When Reb Nison's first son was born, he announced his intention to fulfill his life-long dream of making *aliyah* to *Eretz Yisrael,* but Reb Moshe made it clear that he was not ready to part with his protégé. The Rebbe spoke at the *bris* and said: "It is customary to remark about a great scholar, '*Ehr vachst a Gaon*' (he is growing to become a *Gaon*); regarding Reb Nison, I can tell you that '*ehr iz shoin a Gaon*' (he is already a *Gaon*)." Once again Reb Nison put aside all thoughts of abandoning his beloved Rebbe.

W HEN THE Chevra Bachurim/Bnai Menashe/ Ahavas Achim — better known as the East Third Street Shul — needed a new Rabbi, the thrice-merged congregation offered the position to Rabbi Scheinberg. Reb Chaim Pinchas declined the honor but recommended they hire his new son-in-law instead. The aging congregants, however, were reluctant to hire so youthful a spiritual leader and turned to Reb Moshe for advice. Reb Moshe unhesitatingly added his own endorsement: "Yes, by all means take Reb Nison," he said. "He is a young treasure." They never had cause to regret their choice.

Fortunately, Reb Nison's acceptance of the position was not motivated by promise of financial reward, as the post provided only token remuneration. Despite his lack of means, or perhaps because of it, money meant little to him: no monetary incentive could ever impel him to compromise his principles, and no absence of monetary incentive could deter him from following the dictates of his conscience. Clearly the East Third Street Shul, located in perhaps the most perilous section of the Lower East Side, was unlikely to attract a qualified rabbi, for even the dedicated *mispalelim* had to take their lives in their hands to attend daily services.

Reb Nison served the East Third Street Shul loyally, fearlessly walking alone to the *shtiebel* every day. Reb Moshe frequently made a point of *davening* there just to be near his talmid, and the two would stroll home together undaunted by the very real dangers that lurked all around them. On his way to shul once, Reb Nison sensed a threatening presence behind him. He whirled, raising his arm protectively to ward off the anticipated blow. This reflexive action spared Reb Nison serious injury for his intuition had not deceived him. His attacker, surprised by the intended victim's reaction, swiftly fled — leaving Reb Nison with a very sore arm as a memento of the encounter.

Incidents such as this were far from uncommon as the neighborhood continued to deteriorate. The end finally came when local hooligans set the shul ablaze and the building was reduced to ashes. Reb Nison, the eloquent orator, articulated his congregants' anguish in the *hesped* he delivered over the *shtiebel*'s charred remains:

"If the walls could speak," he intoned with deep emotion, "they would be crying. How many bar mitzvas and *Yiddishe simchas* did we see within our walls! How much learning, how much *davening*..."

One of the worshippers was so moved by the Rabbi's words that he took it upon himself to find a new location for the shul. His efforts did not go unrewarded: he succeeded in securing the cold attic above the Young Israel of the East Side, the very place where Reb Nison learned whenever he felt in danger of drowsing while learning.

Rabbi Alpert viewed this man's achievement as a personal favor and repaid him in a most meaningful way: not long after the relocation of the shul, the man died childless and so Reb Nison took it upon himself to learn the entire *shas* that year *le'illui nishmaso.*

IN 1965 Rabbi Scheinberg made *aliyah* and transplanted his yeshiva to the Mattersdorf neighborhood in Jerusalem. Reb Nison would have joined him but the precarious state of his father's health deterred him from leaving, even though his departure from MTJ at that juncture would not have been viewed as a personal affront to Reb Moshe. By remaining in New York he was able to assist his devoted mother in caring for Reb Shebsel while he continued learning and teaching in the yeshiva.

Reb Nison retained his somewhat less than prestigious teaching position at MTJ for twelve years, despite its stifling nature. When a new opportunity arose, a position which by rights should have been his, again his nonassertive personality and steadfast determination to spare another's feelings — regardless of the personal sacrifice involved — prevailed. The situation, however, was becoming ludicrous: one of the generation's greatest minds and Torah scholars was teaching a group of disinterested preteens.

Rabbi Shmuel Scheinberg, brother of Reb Nison's father-in-law, suggested that Reb Nison apply for a position which had just opened in Yeshivas Rabbeinu Yitzchak Elchonan (Yeshiva University) where he himself taught. The idea was tempting but Reb Nison viewed it with a large measure of skepticism. He was uncertain whether Yeshiva University (YU) could offer him classes more challenging than those where he had been teaching. In deference to Rabbi Scheinberg, however, he applied for the job. '

When he arrived at YU on the day of his interview, he was informed that his interviewer had been unavoidably detained. Thus Reb Nison found himself with several hours "to kill"; predictably, he made his way to the *beis midrash*. The moment he pushed open the door to the study hall was an auspicious one, for it was the turning point of his life.

To Reb Nison's delight, the *beis midrash* of YU reverberated with the welcome, familiar rhythms of Torah study. The earnestness of the *talmidim*'s debates, the intensity of their disputations, the decibel level in the room, were all music to Reb Nison's ears. After consulting Reb Moshe, he accepted the job offered to him and went on to become recognized as one of the outstanding *Roshei Yeshiva* of YU, where he taught and touched the lives of hundreds of loving *talmidim*.

RAV ALPERT (as Reb Nison was known at YU) was like a magnet; all the students, even those who were not regular participants in his *shiur,* were drawn to him. They consulted him on anything and everything, brought him *shailos,* asked him Reb Moshe's opinion. His electrifying *chumash shiurim* drew large crowds of *talmidim* and earned him the acclaim of the entire Torah community.

There was no parallel in the yeshiva world to the ingenuity, conceptualization, incisiveness, pragmatism and wealth of information Rav Alpert exhibited in these *shiurim*. As many tape recorders as students attended the weekly sessions, and the recordings were in great demand. No superlatives can do these *shiurim* justice; they must be heard to be appreciated.

Rabbi Alpert's own *hasmada* was undiminished by the change of venue. With its extensive library of *sifrei kodesh,* YU's *beis midrash* was a treasure trove for him. Day and night, winter and summer, Rav Alpert pursued his studies and examinations of the sacred texts with the diligence for which he was famed. Rebbetzen Alpert once called up Rabbi Zevulun Charlop, the head of the learning program at Yeshiva University, to ask if in fact YU never had an intercession, a vacation, or even a day off.

To Rav Alpert, learning meant being physically present at Sinai: whenever he sensed that something great in the realm of Torah was going on, he felt that he had to be present. [When Rav Alpert visited Israel in 1976 he made a point of attending the renowned Reb Nochum Percowitz's *shiur* in the Mir.] At YU, he frequently attended Rabbi Soloveitchik's *shiur* in order to soak up the Rav's words of wisdom. His presence pleased Rabbi Soloveitchik immensely. Not only did the Rav respect Reb Nison and treasure his words of Torah, he virtually loved him — as did every other *Rosh Yeshiva* with whom Reb Nison came in contact.

Perhaps this was so because of the sheer joy and boyish enthusiasm which radiated from Rav Alpert whenever he heard or uttered a novel interpretation or Torah commentary. Torah was a feast upon which he supped lavishly, but his appetite for learning was never sated.

REB NISON and his family were frequent summer guests of Camp Bais Yaakov. At the end of the season, a van was hired to transport the Alperts and their belongings back to the city. Only after the very last item was secured in the van did Rabbi Alpert interrupt his study to take his seat alongside the driver. And, of course, the moment he sat down he resumed the by then familiar pose always associated with him: an open *sefer* held directly before his eyes. All summer long the campers had ample opportunity to observe this posture and marvel at a man who managed to consume three meals a day in a noisy dining room without ever removing his eyes from a *sefer* or losing his concentration.

One summer, with his passengers safely ensconced in his van, the driver discovered a problem with the vehicle's ignition. The fits and starts of the engine were of little concern to the family squeezed inside, nor to the hundreds of campers and staff members who had gathered to bid farewell to their esteemed guest.

But Rabbi Alpert descended from the van after the third attempt to start the engine. He returned to the spot where he had sat and learned the entire summer, at the foot of a nearby shade tree, with his back toward the van. Throughout the hours-long process of peering under the hood, inspecting this and checking that, Reb Nison did not turn around even once to determine what progress, if any, was being made, despite his eagerness to return home.

Finally, a mechanic was called and a new starter installed — a procedure which generated quite a commotion in the camp. Nevertheless, during more than two hours of continuous disturbance and obvious anxiety, Rabbi Alpert's eyes did not leave his *sefer*. Only when the engine was running at last — a welcome sound to one and all — did Reb Nison resume his seat in the van.

When his dentist informed him that one of his teeth required root canal work, Reb Nison was appalled — but not for the usual reasons. He inquired what the procedure entailed and when he learned that several lengthy sessions were necessary, he asked the dentist to just pull the tooth and be done with it. He simply could not spare the time. For the very same reason he never became a United States citizen: the naturalization process was too time-consuming.

On July 20, 1969 all of America was occupied with one thing and only one thing. Every man, woman and child could be found with eyes riveted to the television screen to witness the event of the century: a fellow American was about to make history by landing on the moon. Those who did not personally own a television crowded around the windows of appliance stores or availed themselves of their friends' hospitality. No one wanted to miss this stirring moment. America was agog with anticipation.

Neighbors rushed into Reb Nison's home (where he was naturally busy learning *gemara*) to tell him that the landing was imminent. His son, who had saved him a seat in a neighbor's living room, hurried in a few minutes later to tell Reb Nison that if he were to come immediately he would not be wasting a second since the "moon walk" was just about to begin.

But, as his son recalls, it wasn't even as though Reb Nison had to battle between natural impulse and a sense of propriety — he simply was not interested. There was nothing that could interest Reb Nison more than a page of *gemara*.

THE TELEPHONE, however, was the one "distraction" to which Reb Nison would respond. This too he had learned from his Rebbe. Who knew what human suffering or personal tragedy awaited his solace at the other end of the phone line? His extensive learning and investigation of Torah, he believed, might increase his own comprehension but could never alter the course of that vast sea of knowledge and wisdom; with one brief word, however, he might change the course of his caller's life. Reb Nison would listen patiently and attentively to all who sought his advice, his sympathy or his encouragement, for what is Torah if not the master blueprint by which mankind constructs the edifice of coexistence on God's earth?

And there was no dearth of callers, both by phone and in person. For each Reb Nison would stop his intense learning and award an attentive ear as though he had nothing else to do. Not all callers, however, were in need of solace. Many, from the thorough ignoramus to the erudite sophist, struck up conversations with Reb Nison for the simple pleasure of speaking to him. He was familiar with an incredible range of disciplines and could converse intelligently — often humorously — on almost any topic. All who approached him were enriched by the experience, for they emerged with a different perspective, a clearer conception, or a new insight that had never before occurred to them — not to mention a few *vertlach* that would surely come in handy one day.

He was a font of knowledge. Students would consult with him about topics to discuss that would impress their dates. On Friday mornings at MTJ Rabbis would line up for Reb Nison to tell them a *drasha* which they could relate to their congregations. He even helped friends write their college theses and for that purpose kept a library of Brooklyn College text books in his bathroom, thereby putting to good use even his time spent there.

This was a man who had enrolled at Washington Irving High School as a raw immigrant with no more than a refugee's command of English, and yet he graduated as valedictorian of his class. Clearly his phenomenal intelligence was not confined to the four walls of the *beis midrash* where, concomitant with his secular studies, he had learned daily and transcribed every *shiur* Reb Moshe delivered.

FAR FROM DAMPENING Reb Nison's high spirits, the academic rigors honed his already sharp sense of humor to a fine point. He once admitted that he hadn't had any "*taam*" in *davening* that morning, then added wryly,

"But at least I have some consolation — I didn't have any *taam* in breakfast either."

Before departing for the Catskill Mountains one year, he removed a handkerchief from his pocket and raised it to Rabbi Siff in the familiar gesture of a *kinyan,* and said, "Here, you can have the East Side for the summer."

A man of very modest means, his wealth of wit was ample compensation. He was once asked how he could afford to take taxis to Yeshiva University, as he did upon occasion. "It is enough that I am a poor man," he replied. "Must I also live like one?"

Reb Nison didn't let his comparatively modest income stand in the way of his natural magnanimity; he was known as a big tipper and could be similarly generous with his time whenever the need arose. As a young boy he escorted an elderly Jew all the way across Manhattan to a hospital where he would receive better treatment than at the local one. Very late at night he could be found delivering money to a penniless Williamsburg family he didn't even know. He often took an emotionally disturbed fellow on walking tours of the Lower East Side and then brought him home to his own house to spend the night.

His generosity of spirit and concern for others were not lost on those who were privileged to have come in contact with him. The disturbed man broke down the door to the Alpert apartment the day the Alperts moved out of the neighborhood. The Gentile tailor who repaired Reb Nison's clothing could not be consoled when he learned of his patron's death. And the list goes on.

HIS REBBE'S unparalleled affection for his fellow Jew expressed itself in many ways. Knowing well what hardships people endured in bearing and raising children, he loved even the offspring of total strangers as though they were his own. Mere mention of the subject of *agunos* brought tears to the *Rosh Yeshiva*'s eyes and he wept uncontrollably at news of the outbreak of World War II for he foresaw the disaster and suffering that were to befall his people.

The capacity to care about the fate and feelings of others is hardly ever acquired or transmitted; humans are usually born with the trait or not. Sensitivity such as Reb Moshe exhibited, however, was rare. In Nison Alpert he found a nature and temperament which mirrored his own, and this reinforced the bond between them. Like his Rebbe, Reb Nison loved his People without regard to their level of religious observance (or nonobservance), country of origin or political bent. When someone once derided secular Israelis, he countered that at least they were prepared to fight for their country, a kind of altruism not apparent in their detractor.

It was Reb Nison's affinity for the Jewish people which compelled him to stand up for their rights and resist any attempts to rob them of their spiritual heritage. When Israeli independence was declared, American Jewry, intoxicated with pride in the nascent state, prepared a warm welcome for David Ben Gurion. On a fundraising mission to the U.S., he was greeted by tens of thousands of supporters at Madison Square Garden in New York. Reb Nison Alpert stood outside picketing against the spiritual genocide which was taking place in Israel under the aegis of the newly-formed government.

For this reason he became one of the founders of Peylim — an organization dedicated to countering attempts to deny Israelis their religious rights and freedom. Reb Nison gave the organization the direction and drive it needed to make the profound impact it has made. He was also the voice of Reb Moshe in the organization, and through Reb Nison, Peylim's active members came to learn who Reb Moshe truly was. As chairman of Peylim's executive board he found no chore too difficult — no task too debasing. He was able to speak with lay people and *Gedolei Yisrael* with the same warmth, *derech eretz,* and when necessary, strength.

In 1963, on an extended visit to *Eretz Yisrael* on behalf of Peylim, he and his close friend Reb Elya Svei met with the local *Gedolim.* These scholars were most impressed with the talmid of Reb Moshe, a young man who was already an outstanding Gaon in his own right. Reb Nison became especially close with Reb Yechezkael Abramsky and the Amshonover Rebbe. Having afforded him the opportunity and privilege of meeting and learning with and from some of the greatest scholars of the era, this trip remained one of the highlights of his life.

That same year, Reb Moshe visited Israel for the *Knessiah Hagedolah* which took place in Jerusalem. Members of an Israeli organization which bears a title similar to Peylim were at odds with the American association, although the latter was founded prior to theirs. They sought an audience with Reb Moshe to air their grievances. Reb Moshe granted the delegation an attentive ear and when they concluded their presentation, Reb Moshe declared: "*Raid nit veggen mein Nison!* " (How dare you speak against my Nison!), thus summarily closing the matter.

Despite his unstinting efforts for Peylim, Reb Nison was circumspect about its achievements. The organization had established numerous schools and a network of youth programs in Israel, yet he realized that so much more was needed to counter the damage. When he again travelled to Israel, in the summer of 1976, and visited the town of Migdal

HaEmek — where Peylim, under the direction of Rav Yitzchak Dovid Grossman, has done its most exemplary work in restoring Sephardic children to religious schools and lifestyles — he was moved to tears. For Reb Nison this was a moment of supreme gratification. After all that had occurred since the early 1950s when Sephardim began immigrating to Israel en masse and were subjected to the invidious assimilation process designed to sever their bonds to their religious and cultural heritage, it was Reb Nison's first opportunity to witness the reversal of that process.

WHILE IN ISRAEL he came across a recently printed *sefer* replete with brilliant *chiddushei Torah* — all plagiarized from him! With remarkable restraint, he quietly confronted the plagiarist and humbly requested that the book be amended. Needless to say, it was.

On matters of *emmes,* however, Reb Nison not only overcame his normally impassive, tolerant nature, but revealed an aggressiveness and intransigence few imagined him to possess. Wherever the honor of Torah or of his Rebbe was at stake he took so uncompromising a stand that none dared oppose him. He once stormed into a conference room in the midst of a meeting of the *Agudas Harabbanim* and banged forcefully on the table to register his objection. When a council of which he was a member exceeded the limits on a particular issue, he disavowed all association with the organization and protested publicly. His students at YU were tremendously impressed by his equanimity; the one thing which truly incensed him was the reliance on or citation of dubious halakhic leniencies. Only for an issue of Torah could he overcome his innate humility.

Rebbetzen Alpert claims that in all their years together

she heard her husband utter only one statement which might be construed as lacking humility. When the Alperts' apartment was being repainted — a job which is an unpleasant necessity for a conscientious housekeeper like Rebbetzen Alpert but a thoroughly pointless nuisance for a devoted scholar — the Rebbetzen wished to limit the *bitul Torah* her husband would be forced to suffer. She therefore offered to remove his countless *sefarim* from their shelves herself and asked if he would be able to remember their proper sequence and location when it was time to replace them. Reb Nison replied with this, his haughtiest statement: "Blindfolded, I would know which are my *sefarim* and where they belong."

REB NISON was content with his modest income and never harbored aspirations to become a prominent Rabbi of a distinguished congregation, until Reb Moshe told him the time had come for him to serve the public. The Agudas Yisrael Shul in Far Rockaway, New York, a congregation comprised largely of yeshiva graduates and learned *baalei battim,* was in need of a new rabbi and had turned to Reb Moshe for a recommendation.

For a discerning congregation such as that of the Agudas Yisrael Shul, no ordinary God-fearing cleric would suffice; only a genuine scholar and inspiring leader could meet the demands of the community. Their choice and hope was Nison Alpert. And they were not disappointed.

Local cynics, who had seen numerous Rabbis come and go, at first gave him an icy reception but soon even they melted in admiration for their new Rav. In no time at all, Rav Alpert earned the respect and even reverence of every member of the shul.

When he first accepted the position, he was still living on

the Lower East Side, a considerable distance from Far Rockaway. This situation, it was assumed, was only temporary. In fact, it lasted for more than three years. Every Tuesday and Thursday evening Rav Alpert would make the tiring, often hazardous journey from lower Manhattan to Long Island by train — as he neither owned a car nor knew how to drive — in order to deliver the biweekly *shiur.* To him the long trips were no more than a minor inconvenience. Inclement weather, train delays, hoodlums and the like were obstacles which he simply had to overcome; his obligation to the community was foremost. If the *baalei battim* had required a greater incentive for attendance than the sheer brilliance, the depth of analysis and the immense enjoyability of the *shiurim,* they found it in their Rav's dependable, inexhaustible constancy.

On one freezing winter night, when well over a foot of snow had fallen, the *baalei battim* saw no need to determine whether or not the *shiur* would be cancelled that evening; if even local trips were not attempted on a night such as this unless they were absolutely vital, surely the Rabbi had stayed at home.

Looking out his window to see if the snowstorm had ended, Moshe Hirth, a dedicated *shiur*-participant, happened to notice that the shul lights were on. Could there be a robbery in progress, he wondered, or were vandals at work? Bundled up against the storm, he braved the weather to investigate. To his astonishment, Hirth found Rav Alpert sitting and learning and waiting expectantly at the *shiur* table.

"Rebbe!" Hirth exclaimed. "You needn't have come on a night like this. We could all have learned by ourselves!" Rav Alpert, whose sense of humor remained warm despite the cold, responded, "That's what I was afraid of!"

As Rabbi of the shul, his presence on Shabbos was

naturally expected. Arrangements were made for him to spend each Shabbos as the guest of one of the congregants until his anticipated move to the neighborhood. No one imagined this arrangement would continue for over three years.

Every weekend he would stay with a different family, never expressing a preference, or reciting *kiddush* or *hamotzi* unless the host insisted. He made no inquiries beforehand concerning the family's level of observance, nor abstained from eating certain dishes. This effort to avoid embarrassing anyone resulted, on occasion, in his having to eat at homes where the degree of modesty observed was below par and some of the family's practices might have made others — of far lesser stature than Rav Alpert — reluctant to eat there.

By the time the next snowstorm struck New York, on the shortest *erev* Shabbos of the year, the Agudas Yisrael congregants knew their Rav would not be deterred. A yeshiva student was therefore dispatched to Manhattan to bring the Rav to Far Rockaway by car. As the young man and his Rav rode along the expressway, however, the storm became even more severe and driving conditions deteriorated until it was impossible to continue. A few miles out of Far Rockaway, they surrendered to *force majeure* and pulled into a cargo terminal at Kennedy International Airport to spend the most enlightening, inspiring and memorable Shabbos in that student's life.

RABBI ALPERT was the ideal Shabbos guest. He brought to his host's home an endless array of *divrei Torah,* enlightening conversation, heartfelt compliments to the hostess, and his own natural warmth. He never disregarded the other family members and guests sitting around the table, but pointedly included them in discussions and evinced a sincere interest in their occupations and studies.

One Shabbos, he noticed that his host's daughter seemed unusually nervous. "What's troubling you?" the Rav asked. "I have an important history exam this week," she lamented, "and I don't know a thing." "Don't worry," the Rav reassured her, "I will help you study." And he did.

At the home of another family one of the younger children was crying incessantly, to the consternation of Rav Alpert's hosts. Without a moment's hesitation, he lifted up the toddler and sat him on his lap. "If I will buy you a toy, will you stop crying?" the Rav asked. The child immediately stopped crying and nodded his agreement. The next *erev* Shabbos, Rabbi Alpert made a point of stopping off at the home of that same family and personally handing the child the toy that he had bought.

Throughout this protracted period, Rabbi Alpert continued to shuttle from house to house with no place to call his own. He even occasionally suffered the humiliation, through quirk of fate or oversight, of finding himself with no host at all. More than once, he saw his intended host walk out of shul without waiting for him, an indication that some error had been made. And then, like a homeless vagabond, he would be compelled to knock on someone's door seeking bed and board for the weekend.

The Alperts' relentless search for a suitable house in the neighborhood became a source of unending frustration and disappointment. In a stable community such as Far Rockaway, few decent homes come on the market and their choice seemed limited to ramshackle structures crumbling to ruins or rambling mansions the price and upkeep of which were astronomical. To a man for whom a cot and a *sefer* would have sufficed, having to continue imposing on the hospitality of his *baalei battim* was more than awkward; it was outrageous exploitation. Sympathizing with Rav Alpert's plight, the congregants went out of their way to make him feel welcome and convince him that, far from being an imposition, his weekly presence in their homes was a privilege. Their kindness prompted Rav Alpert to comment sardonically: "I don't need a home — I need fifty-two *baalei battim.*"

As Rav of the shul he set an example for the entire community. He served as a *dayan* to adjudicate *dinei Torah,* but far more often, the moment he learned of a dispute he would try and resolve it quietly without it ever becoming publicly known.

The *baalei battim* took pride in their Rabbi's *hasmada:* it gave them a sense of living within a yeshiva. They noticed that every day, when Rav Alpert returned home from Yeshivas Rabbeinu Yitzchak Elchanan, instead of getting off the bus at his house, he continued directly to the shul. The lights there would burn late into the night while their Rabbi diligently learned Torah. It provided a wonderful feeling of security to know that the Rav was available to all who might seek his counsel, even while most of the neighborhood slept.

Those who did seek his advice — and there were many — had good cause to cherish it. The aging and ailing Reb Moshe had retired to virtual seclusion, inaccessible to his myriad followers, and so Rav Alpert became the voice of the Gaon to the general public. All who wished to know Reb Moshe's opinion on an issue, asked his talmid, the man who had heard his Rebbe's *piskei halacha* first-hand.

I N 1983 the Alperts suffered a terrible loss. Their beloved son, Yishaya Mendel (Shaya), a child possessed of such unusual physical beauty and outstanding *middos* that he was adored by all who set eyes upon him, developed an aneurism, a fatal enlargement of a blood vessel in the brain. With his son's life hanging by a thread, Rav Alpert tried desperately to intercede in Heaven on Shaya's behalf, but he did not have the heart to tell his Rebbe of his son's plight. He knew that Reb Moshe, who was often tended by Shaya, would be devastated and would immediately decree a public fast, but the dreadful news was sure to have a detrimental effect on the Gaon's own fragile state of health.

Rabbi Mordechai Tendler, Reb Moshe's grandson and devoted aide, succeeded in keeping the news from the *Rosh Yeshiva* until the day that Shaya Alpert returned his unblemished soul to his Maker. Only when the hour of the funeral was approaching and Reb Mordechai had to excuse himself from the house in order to attend, did he reveal to his grandfather the tragic tidings.

The *Rosh Yeshiva,* bedridden with a host of medical problems the least of which was excruciating sciatica, immediately telephoned his son, Reb Reuven, to have him arrange a ride to the *levaya.* Reb Reuven offered every excuse that came to mind ("There are no taxis available," "The roads are blocked," etc.) to prevent his venerable, ailing father from leaving the house, knowing how injurious the effort might be.

Through resourcefulness and sheer determination, Reb Moshe made his own arrangements, arriving at the funeral just as Rav Alpert was delivering the eulogy for his treasured child. The Rebbe's entrance, heralded by a burly New York City policeman shouting, "Clear the way, clear the way for Reb Moshe!" was awe-inspiring.

Rav Alpert looked up and saw his Rebbe. "*Zest, Shaya?* " he whispered reverently. "*Di Rosh Yeshiva iz gekummen melava zein.*" (See, my dear son? The *Rosh Yeshiva* has come to escort you.)

Rav Alpert, despite his overwhelming grief, was still able to think about others, even at the very moment of the funeral procession. It was then that he noticed a congregant of his shul whom he had not seen for several weeks and to whom he had promised a donation for a worthy cause. Rabbi Alpert's behavior was typical of a man who genuinely practiced what he preached, for indeed he had often spoken on the subject of acceptance of God's will, regardless of the degree of pain and suffering.

Just as Shaya's coffin was being escorted from the yeshiva, Rav Alpert turned to his congregant and said: "I have the check waiting for you, only I don't have it on me right now."

IN 1985 Reb Nison started to feel sharp pains in his shoulder and back. He could not know then how severe the problem was, but he neither complained nor deviated from his rigorous learning schedule. He only begged people's indulgence whenever the pain caused his body to contort or when he remained seated while speaking to them.

It was not until the following autumn that his problem was diagnosed as more than serious. Horror and dismay spread throughout the Torah world, and Reb Moshe proclaimed a day of fasting on behalf of his precious talmid. Who can say what superhuman endurance it required, but the fact is that Reb Nison did not miss a single *shiur* or hour in the *beis midrash* while this pernicious disease raged on, spreading rapidly throughout his body. No one knew the agonies he suffered; the only time away from his learning was time spent with radiology and chemotherapy treatments.

He would hurry from the hospital to his *shiur* in YU, apologizing to his students for the large bandages covering his forehead — reminders of the treatments he had just undergone — and begging that they not be alarmed. Still without a car and with the added awesome burden of his terrible illness, he continued to adhere to the same arduous, impossible routine of previous years. He lived in Far Rockaway and delivered *shiurim* there; he was a *gemara rebbe* in YU in Upper Manhattan and director of the Yeshiva's *Yadin Yadin Kollel;* and yet, at almost any given time, even very late at night, he could be found in the *beis midrash* at MTJ, sitting and learning.

Everyone was aware of the gravity of the situation, and it was not long before the effects of the disease and the treatments became apparent, yet whenever Rav Alpert was asked how he was feeling, he would reply in the same high spirits as he always had, with a blessing to his Creator on his tongue and a smile on his lips.

When he was confined to the hospital for extensive treatments, he managed to escape each evening to *daven Maariv* at MTJ, with the hospital bracelet still around his wrist. And, naturally, since he was already in the *beis midrash,* he seized the opportunity to learn a little as well. Needless to say, the sight of Rav Alpert learning deep into the night, wearing a sublime smile of inner peace and a hospital bracelet, left a lasting impression on all those present fortunate enough to be in better health.

But even in the hospital and during the treatments nothing could keep Rav Alpert from learning. Before he underwent a CAT scan, a congregant who had escorted him saw Rav Alpert's face light up with glee. The CAT scan, known to be a most unnerving experience, was unlikely to cause the Rav such joy, but before the congregant could express his bewilderment, Rav Alpert instructed him to tell Mr. Ploni that he had figured out an answer to Ploni's question concerning the Sephardic custom for *naanuim.* At times when most people would be entirely self-absorbed, Rav Alpert was absorbed only in Torah. He asked anyone who accompanied him to the hospital to share a *chiddush* with him.

Not only did he not neglect his own learning during that trying time, he also did not forget his friends or the communal responsibilities he had shouldered. When a boy from his shul with whom he had a close relationship became engaged, he once again went AWOL from the hospital to attend the *simcha.* His repeated disappearances from the hospital, perpetrated against the express wishes of his family and instructions of his doctors, precluded his travelling with an escort, and so, alone, he made the long journey to where the engagement party was being held. Such was his loyalty and devotion to a friend.

RAV ALPERT'S attitude towards the various respon- sibilities he had asssumed was no different. One of his final public appearances was at a parlor meeting to raise money on behalf of Peylim. It took a considerable amount of influence for the intended host to agree to open his house for the meeting, but Rav Alpert succeeded in convincing him at last.

By the time of this meeting, Rav Alpert's health was so tenuous that it pained people just to look at him. A mere shadow of his former, robust self, he was barely able to speak without succumbing to violent coughing fits. Amazingly, however, whenever he would deliver a *shiur* or speak words of Torah, he was spared the bone-jarring, uncontrollable coughing spasms.

Notwithstanding his physical condition, his mind and his wit were as sharp as ever. A hush fell over the audience as he opened the meeting. His voice was very low, almost inaudible, and every word was evidently labored. "When I was younger," he began. "I used to dabble quite a bit in *shidduchim*..."

As usual, Rav Alpert's words managed to evoke a smile from all those assembled and to shift the rather somber mood. "Although I never really accomplished very much in that realm," he continued, "there is one *shidduch* of which I am extremely proud." By this point Rav Alpert had totally altered the focus of the evening, and completely captivated his audience. He was well aware of this, but still was not tempted to use the podium to utter witticisms by which he knew he would be remembered, for he was certain this was to be one of his last talks. He had personally gathered everyone together that evening, in the home of an initially reluctant host, in the hope that they would part with their hard-earned money for a vital cause and he could not be diverted from this objective.

After pausing to allow his words to have greater impact, he concluded: "And that *shidduch,* is our host and the purpose for which we have convened here tonight."

The eyes of all present swam with tears. "Rebbe," the host declared, "I promise to provide my house next year, and the year after that — as long as you wish — for this cause, if you will only promise to be here with us to open our meetings."

Rav Alpert wished he could have made that promise. No one wished to live more than he. The next few nights, in the bitter cold, counter to the wishes and insistence of all those who cared about him, Rav Alpert devoted his attention to a new cause. Together with his friend, Reb Dov Wallowitz, and Rabbi Meir Shuster of Jerusalem, he trudged through the snow to collect money for the fight against assimilation. On one of those nights, when it was snowing particularly hard, Reb Dov urged Rav Alpert to turn back. To Rav

Alpert, however, his personal well-being was of far lesser consequence than an issue so essential to *Klal Yisrael.*

Rav Alpert's self-sacrifice was not lost on the people upon whose doors he knocked. Seeing him out in the cold, his irresistible humor punctuated by dreadful coughing, made their hearts melt and they all gave generously.

REB NISON'S NAME, it has been said, foreshadowed a life filled with *nisyonos* — trials and tribulations which would have destroyed a lesser man: a childhood and youth of poverty; a father incapacitated by illness throughout his son's formative years; a degrading job for which he was underpaid and his enormous talents underutilized; the tragic loss of his teenage son; his own appalling disease. But one of the greatest *nisyonos* Rav Alpert had to endure was the passing of his revered Rebbe on *erev* Purim 5746. He was asked to eulogize Reb Moshe at the funeral, and his *hesped* was so stirring that one wonders if ever a talmid bade farewell to his Rebbe more eloquently.

From the time of Reb Moshe's passing, Rav Alpert's own deterioration accelerated. His congregants sensed that the Rav's *Shabbos HaGadol drashah* would be his last and it was attended en masse. He delivered his *drashah* before a standing-room-only crowd; men, women and children strained to hear and absorb their esteemed Rav's final address. And Rav Alpert, the gifted orator who always knew what to say and how to say it in the most appealing way, truly outdid himself on that Shabbos afternoon. It was a *drashah* that will long be remembered.

By *chol haMoed* Pesach, his condition was grave. His loving followers stormed the gates of Heaven with their supplications and devoted *talmidim* in Israel congregated at the *Kosel* to pray for their dear Rebbe. In BYA seminary in Brooklyn, where Rav Alpert's youngest daughter teaches, classes were suspended so that students could recite *Tehillim*. On *Rosh Chodesh Iyar,* the Jews of Far Rockaway crowded into the Agudas Yisrael shul, crammed the adjacent alley and overflowed onto the street to add their voices and heartfelt prayers.

Rabbi Alpert was transferred to the home of his dear son-in-law, Rabbi Dovid Weinberger, where loving care was constantly provided. It was Reb Dovid who led the family at this difficult time, and with the help of his wife and friends in the community, he did his utmost to spare the Rebbetzen any additional grief.

THIS WAS THE MOST difficult phase of Rabbi Alpert's existence, but not only for the obvious reasons. When, earlier, he had been compelled to regularly undergo excruciating radiology treatments, his usually jovial spirits began to sag. His close friend, Reb Dov Wallowitz, who had escorted him to Boston for the treatments, had implored Reb Nison to unburden himself. Rabbi Alpert had always been such a happy, friendly individual — it seemed strange that after all he had gone through with his illness and still had carried on as if nothing was wrong, that suddenly he should appear so despondent.

"Dov," Reb Nison had said, fighting back the tears, "it is the *bitul Torah* which is killing me."

How much more trying it must have been for him to discover that even the strength to hold a *sefer* had abandoned him? Yet, in this horribly debilitated state, Rav Alpert was unwilling to forego the joy of Torah study. Unable to manage on his own, he had his daughter sit at his bedside and read to him from a *chumash*.

The Rav knew he was dying but he would not release his grip on life without a battle. Every minute more that he held on was a minute more of learning or a minute more of performing *mitzvos*. Three times the dedicated HATZOLOH emergency medical team — in constant attendance — succeeded in reviving him. In all their experience, the rescuers claim, they never saw a man who wanted so desperately to live.

And each time, after the HATZOLOH members' arduous efforts successfully restabilized the Rav's condition, he raised his hand in a salute of thanks or with his gentle eyes acknowledged his gratitude. Throughout this period, as in the earlier stages of his illness, Rabbi Alpert was meticulous about expressing appreciation for even the most minor service rendered and for even the most discomforting though essential tasks performed on his behalf. Despite the intravenous solutions that dripped steadily into his veins and the oxygen that eased his labored breathing, the lessons he had learned from his Rebbe were not forgotten.

Towards the end of Reb Moshe's life, the *Rosh Yeshiva* had to undergo a biopsy — a painful test which involves the insertion of a long needle, filled with a tiny shovel-like tip, deep into the body in order to remove a tissue sample. Prior to this test, Reb Moshe had endured without protest batteries of tests and numerous procedures that were not only painful but degrading as well. This particular test, however, Reb Moshe found too agonizing to bear, and asked the medical technician to remove the needle.

Over his patient's protests, the technician continued to jab deeper, assuring Reb Moshe that the procedure would take only a few more seconds. It is not uncommon for hospital staff to become inured to patients' complaints, particularly when a test performed routinely is known to be painful but is essential for diagnostic purposes.

"I suppose you didn't hear the Rabbi," Reb Moshe's son-in-law intervened, and physically withdrew the technician's hand. Surprised, but unwilling to counter the authoritative voice of Rabbi Moshe Tendler, the technician packed his samples and paraphernalia and prepared to leave. Just then, Reb Moshe's attendant informed him that the Rabbi wished to speak to him. The medical technician was certain the Rabbi intended to upbraid him personally for having caused him discomfort and for attempting to continue against his will. Reb Moshe, however, had something else in mind. Through an interpreter, he conveyed to the technician his gratitude for the service rendered. "I understand that you were only doing your job and trying your hardest."

THE ALPERT FAMILY always said that Rav Alpert "lived for his *talmidim*." Never was that more apparent than at the end of his days. It was to be the last Friday of his life, and his agony and torment were registered clearly on his withered countenance. The previous night had been a most demanding one for the HATZOLOH members and *Tehillim* reciters alike, as the thin thread by which Rav Alpert clung to life unraveled. Suddenly, a talmid who had just arrived from *Eretz Yisrael* entered the Rav's room, bringing tidings and good wishes from the Holy Land.

To the utter amazement of all those present, Rav Alpert, somehow, raised himself up in his bed. An electrifying smile lit up his face and he greeted the young man with a hearty "*Shalom Aleichem*" such as had not been heard from the Rav in many months. Family and friends rushed in to witness this precious scene: a Rebbe in his final hours deriving *nachas* from a talmid.*

* The author was the talmid who was privileged to bring his Rebbe greetings from *Eretz Yisrael* and a modicum of pleasure at the end of his days.

Later that day, a friend and congregant whose son was to be married the following week was allowed entrance in order to receive the Rav's blessing. Rav Alpert clasped his hand and uttered seven words: *"Bitachon,* Reb Shimon! *Bitachon* Reb Shimon! *Bitachon."*

Rav Alpert's use of the term *"bitachon"* did not mean, simply, "trust in God that all will go well." He was alluding rather to the explanation of the Chazon Ish for *"bitachon"*, an explanation he had cited often: "Trust in God, for all that He does is good."

And in the last hours of Rav Alpert's life, when he was too weak to speak or even to move his limbs, a student tried to communicate with him by reciting the *aleph-beis* and watching for a reaction to any particular letter. His loving family, students, congregants and Jews the world over longed for one final message, one word to help them carry on in a world that would be so empty and dark after his departure. The Rav found the strength to comply.

At the letter *"beis"* he gave a sign; again at the letter *"tes."* There was no reaction to any other letter, but the student felt certain that his Rav wanted to convey something of import, so he did not give up. He went through the alphabet one more time. Now at *"ches"* another flutter was perceived, and at *"nun"* Rav Alpert made his last voluntary movement.

"ב ט ח נ"

"Bitachon", have faith, for everything — even suffering — is God's will and is therefore good. He had once explained suffering, referring to our subjugation in Egypt, as a form of preparation for a spiritual experience. Suffering, Rav Alpert had said, strips away any haughtiness, any ego or feelings of self-importance which may stand in the way of God's message entering the heart.

Clearly Rav Alpert suffered sufficiently to entitle him to the spiritual experience and delight of resuming to learn with his father, his son Shaya and his revered Rebbe, Reb Moshe. No doubt they, and the Chafetz Chaim (to whom he was related) and the Meiri (whose manuscript he had published) and the Raavad (whose manuscript he had prepared for publication) were all waiting to greet him with joy, deference and love.

RAV ALPERT once discussed the discrepancy between the version in the *gemara Chagiga* and the text in the *Midrash* on *Shir HaShirim* regarding the four who entered PARDES: Four of the greatest scholars ever penetrated the inner sanctums of the Torah's secrets and three of them were adversely affected. Rabi Akiva, however, "*yatza beshalom,*" came out whole and in peace.

Why was Rabi Akiva privileged to come out of PARDES unscathed? Rabbi Alpert explained that the version in the *Midrash* provides the solution. There it says: "*Rabi Akiva nichnas beshalom veyatza beshalom,*" Rabi Akiva entered in peace and, therefore, came out in peace.

"How does one avoid *machlokes* and strife?" asked Rav Alpert. By emulating Rabi Akiva. If one approaches all problems in peace then one will resolve them in peace. Rav Alpert was the embodiment of this concept. Time and again his mere presence in a room full of disputing parties had been sufficient to bring about a peaceable solution. Little wonder that he was called upon so often to settle quarrels and resolve disputes. Since Reb Nison always "*nichnas beshalom*", had always entered in peace, he left in peace as well.

Not long before Reb Moshe's passing the great Rebbe commented: "*Dacht sach mir, az in mien ganze lebben hob ich kein mohl nit aimetzen vey getohn.*" (I don't believe that I ever caused anyone any harm all my life.) His talmid, with the same humility, could have uttered the same incredible declaration.

It was so evident that Rav Alpert could not remain in this world without his Rebbe, that people could not help but notice the contrast between his state of health before and after Reb Moshe's passing. He had followed his Rebbe's example in every respect throughout his lifetime. And now, once again, for the final, most tragic time, the talmid was to follow his Rebbe.

O N SUNDAY EVENING, the Seventeenth of *Iyar,* 5746, Reb Nison Alpert's soul was summoned to the Heavenly Assembly. The secular date was Memorial Day, a legal holiday which would enable thousands of Jews to come and bid farewell to the great talmid.

A funeral service was held at Yeshiva University early in the morning, where over eight hundred students interrupted their studying for final examinations to pay their last respects to the man whom they had cherished so much.

The funeral then proceeded to Mesivta Tiferes Yerushalayim on New York's Lower East Side. Once again Reb Nison returned to his favorite house of study, this time to be himself honored in the *beis midrash* he had honored and graced by his presence. Reb Nison was no stranger to the residents of the East Side: They had watched this "local boy" grow to greatness under the aegis and with the encouragement of their very own Gaon. Reb Moshe's love for Nison Alpert would have been adequate justification for East Siders to open their hearts to him, but "Johnny," with his affable charm and prodigious scholarship, had endeared himself to them and had made them proud to have been his neighbors. They attended his funeral en masse, joined by hundreds of students who knew precisely how they could best spend their day off from school.

The New York City Police Department was also well represented but in far greater numbers than would have appeared necessary for simply cordoning off the long block where MTJ is located. When he lived on the East Side, Rabbi Alpert had served as chaplain of the local police precinct.

There was one young patrolman back in those days who took a special liking to Rav Alpert; his name was Webber. A Jew who had made it up through the police ranks, Lieutenant Webber had never forgotten his Rabbi: every Simchas Torah he appeared at Rabbi Alpert's shul and danced with the Rav.

Lieutenant Webber had eventually become Captain Webber, Chief of Police of Far Rockaway. When he learned, at seven o'clock in the morning on Memorial Day, of his Rabbi's demise, he rushed to the Alpert home to offer his condolences and his assistance.

The Police Chief saw to it that this *borayach min hakavod* (fleer from honor) was awarded the final honor. An armada of New York's mobile units was dispatched to ensure that the funeral procession would travel uninterrupted on the final leg of the journey in Far Rockaway. From there, the coffin was to be flown to a massive funeral in Jerusalem prior to burial on *Har Hazeisim,* alongside Reb Nison's son and father. New York's major arteries and superhighways, notorious for their congestion and monumental traffic jams, were cleared of every vehicle as highway patrolmen and motorcycle police kept the access lanes bottled up in the sizzling heat — all to allow free passage for the funeral procession.

The entire Far Rockaway Jewish community attended a funeral service the likes of which the town had never seen. They came to mourn their Rabbi, lament the sorry lot of world Jewry at large, and acknowledge that with Rav Nison Alpert's passing the hope of finding an immediate and fitting successor to Reb Moshe died as well.

Eulogies

EULOGY
for Harav Hagaon
Reb Moshe Feinstein zt"l

delivered at Mesivta Tiferes Yerushalayim, NY

by Reb Nison Alpert zt"l

When Reb Elazar, the disciple of Reb Yochanan, became ill, the master came to visit him. As soon as Reb Yochanan entered his student's home, he was appalled by the total absence of light in the house. He raised his sleeve, exposing his hand, and the house became illuminated.

Reb Yochanan then turned to his disciple who was crying and asked, "Why do you cry, my son? Because of your poverty, or perhaps because of the untimely death of your children?"

"No, my master," responded Reb Elazar. "I am crying neither for my poverty nor for any misfortune of mine. Rather, I am crying for you. I cry because of the realization that one day beauty such as yours will decay in the ground."

How astounding! Reb Yochanan is alive and well, instructing and leading the Jewish people, yet his disciple Reb Elazar eulogizes him. What could have provoked this bizarre feeling of bereavement and loss?

The answer is that if a man of stature passes away, but leaves a worthy successor to carry on after him, his beauty will not decay. Even though the Rebbe has died, his beauty continues to shine forth and illuminate the world via his disciples and followers. Reb Elazar was such a close disciple of Reb Yochanan that he was painfully aware of his Rebbe's brilliance and the vacuum which would follow it. Reb Yochanan's beauty was destined to decay in the ground.

I have been asked, as the disciple of Reb Moshe, to eulogize him. As a disciple who has spent so many years in his majestic company, and witnessed, to just a small degree, the radiance and nobility that were his, I can only weep. Woe to this beauty that shall now decay! It is gone with none to replace it. Let us try to recapture some of that radiance, that I was privileged to glimpse as a disciple.

The *Rosh Yeshiva* accepted me into the yeshiva when I was thirteen years old. He would wake up at two o'clock in the morning on Fridays in order to prepare the *pilpul shiur* which he would deliver later that day [the collection of which were subsequently printed in the *Dibros Moshe*]. Over twenty questions were asked on each *sugya* or topic encompassing all of the major points. He would then establish two fundamental approaches, which would subdivide further, to unravel and solve all of the difficulties raised.

Only after this would he leave for *Shacharis,* eat breakfast, and then return to the *shiur*'s preparation by locking himself up in a room for two hours. At this time he would review the discourse by heart, and finally deliver the two-hour *shiur* at eleven o'clock.

Everyone hurried out after the *shiur,* especially on the short winter Fridays. Reb Moshe, however, would remain to put away the *sefarim* and turn off the lights (which often entailed standing on a chair or table to reach the cord switch). I began to help my Rebbe put away the *sefarim* and carry home his belongings and our relationship grew until I became a virtual member of the household. This enabled me to witness not only isolated manifestations of his greatness, but rather deliberate behavior patterns and Torah perspectives on life.

A most distinguished person once asked me why Reb Moshe consents to write letters of support for every organization and individual who approaches him. "Doesn't he realize that he is thus cheapening himself?" the man inquired. Reb Moshe was well aware of the little regard people accorded his letters. He once asked a prospective recipient of an endorsement, "Honestly, how can my letter help you? I've written thousands of similar ones!"

"At least," the fellow continued, "he should investigate to determine if their stories and needs are really true."

I responded that we find the terms *"chessed"*

and "*emmes*" juxtaposed frequently in the Torah, yet *chessed* is always written first. If a man begins with *chessed* (kindness), tempering it with truth, good is likely to come of it. However, if he begins with "truth," he will never come to *chessed* — and who knows how true his *emmes* will be?

This was clearly a guiding principle for Reb Moshe. Whenever someone was in need, he would do whatever possible to help, before weighing any other considerations. Likewise he was a man who was the very embodiment of peace. No effort was too great for him to try and unite disputing parties. Sometimes this even entailed overlooking things not in accord with his perspective, but it would not deter him.

Someone once described Reb Moshe as a *Gadol* "possessing nothing exceptional." He meant that if there is something extraordinary about a person it is immediately noticed. An exceptionally long arm, for example, is immediately noticed, whereas when everything is proportionate and symmetrical it escapes observation.

When a person excels in one particular area, it is this incongruity which causes attention. But what "stood out" about Reb Moshe? His brilliance was matched by his diligence, the nature of his observance by his kindness, the warmth of his emotions and davening by the coldness of his analytical reasoning. He was the *shlaimus* of *shlaimus* — a totality of perfection.

When I returned home last night from a few *simchas* I learned the tragic news of the *Rosh Yeshiva*'s passing. Memories began to flash back and I remembered escorting Reb Moshe to three weddings in a single night. We began at Ninetieth Street and then travelled downtown to the Broadway Central before leaving for Flatbush. After the third wedding we returned to the first one where they were just beginning *bircas hamazon*. Both of us were tired, hungry and thoroughly exhausted, yet Reb Moshe realized how much joy his presence brought to the groom. I remarked to the *Rosh Yeshiva* that there is an expression, "You can't dance at two weddings," but the *Rosh Yeshiva* managed to dance at three!

A *chassan* once invited him to attend his wedding. Reb Moshe was rather surprised since he had never met the groom before. The groom conceded the point but explained that he was marrying a Sephardic girl and was afraid that several halakhic problems may arise regarding the *kesuba* (marriage contract). Reb Moshe attended the wedding, not as the *mesader kiddushin* (officiating rabbi) or to receive any other honor — merely to put the groom at ease.

These stories are of no meaning unless we understand the paramount value time had for him. I remember the day that Rav Shisgal, his son-in-law, died. Reb Moshe returned home from the hospital at about ten o'clock at night, and was awakened at midnight and informed of the passing. I woke up early the next morning and saw Reb Moshe already out on his porch writing his *chiddushei Torah*. He realized that he would not be able to write on that day and therefore tried to get in whatever he could. Reb Moshe would not sacrifice "time" for his own personal bereavement, yet gave it away to gladden a groom he had never met.

I wish to conclude with the *Rosh Yeshiva*'s own words, that which he said on the occasion of the funeral of Reb Aharon Cohen, the *Rosh Yeshiva* of Chevron: The Prophet Malachi describes Aaron the Priest with the words: "A Torah of truth was in his mouth, and no iniquity crossed his lips."

Reb Moshe asked what is praiseworthy about the fact that Aaron did not use evil language? Would we have expected otherwise? He answered that even when Aaron was rebuking a sinner, he had no need to relate to the evil deed itself. Any sinner who would witness Aaron in his majesty and purity would automatically repent of his own accord.

How fitting are these words to describe Reb Moshe himself. Mean words never crossed his lips, nor did they have to. To behold Reb Moshe, to view him in his majesty, purity, holiness, righteousness, kindness, humility and rapture, precluded the need for any admonishment. Without rebuking, the sinner felt rebuked. His personality, his very being was a living *mussar sefer*.

The Talmud relates an incident about the women of Shchentziv who eulogized. Why was it that the women eulogized instead of the more prominent people? The answer is that not everything can be explained rationally and intellectually, or with the rhetoric sometimes found within a eulogy.

The acute pain and suffering can be best expressed through the simple, unaffected words of a woman. Instead of describing Reb Moshe I would much prefer to call out to him, "Rebbe, Rebbe to whom have you abandoned us? We are orphans without a home or a leader. What will become of us?"

Reb Moshe's last words were "I have no strength left." As long as he could, he battled his illness with herculean strength, realizing full well that the responsibility of *Klal Yisrael* rested on his frail shoulders. And when he could no longer bear this awesome yoke, he left us...

Returning to the story of Reb Elazar and Reb Yochanan, the *gemara* relates that after they both sat and sobbed for a while, Reb Yochanan stretched out his hand to his disciple Reb Elazar and lifted him up, simultaneously curing him of his illness.

Rebbe, Rebbe, stretch out a hand from that great abyss which separates us. Lift us up that we may be healed from our sickness and squalor... all of us, your family, your disciples, and the entire Jewish Nation.

EULOGY
for Harav Hagaon
Reb Moshe Feinstein zt"l

delivered at Agudas Yisrael Shul, Far Rockaway, NY
by Reb Nison Alpert zt"l

The *Rosh Yeshiva* was imbued with rare talents. Not only did he never forget anything he learned, but he once told me that it was beyond him how people *could* forget!

The Torah says: "I have selected Bezalel son of Uri son of Chur, of the tribe of Yehuda, by name. I have filled him with a Divine spirit, with wisdom, understanding and knowledge, and with the talent for all types of craftsmanship" (Shmos 31:2,3). This verse alludes to the fact that God Himself was actually campaigning on behalf of Bezalel. One may not lead a community without its consent, and that was precisely what God was trying to elicit: the agreement and recognition by Bnei Yisrael of Bezalel as the most qualified architect in the nation. Part of God's strategy was to endow him with "the spirit of the Lord."

The purpose of this spirit, of the various talents which Bezalel possessed, was not to enable him to become a gifted businessman, or to enable him to amass vast sums of money. He was endowed with the Divine spirit in the realm of wisdom, understanding and knowledge. In other words, the purpose of the spirit was to dedicate it solely to the service of God.

And since Bezalel had these talents and abilities, he was the natural choice, the Divine choice, to be the architect of God's *mishkan*. The *Rosh Yeshiva* was given talents and he used them to lead the nation.

In keeping with his modest nature, the *Rosh Yeshiva* rarely referred to his talents, but there was one thing which he related to me and to others. He said: "I have never wasted time."

A friend of the *Rosh Yeshiva*'s from the First World War recalled how once during the war a heated argument arose about the situation at the battlefront. At the time it was not even clear who was winning the war. The *Rosh Yeshiva,* who was present throughout the entire conversation, did not participate in the discussion. Oblivious to the dialogue, he continued to learn and write, for every second was precious. Every moment was needed for preparing to serve the Jewish nation.

Indeed, a great scholar who used to record everything which the *Rosh Yeshiva* said, once complained to Reb Moshe's Rebbetzen for allowing him to lie down to take a rest on Shabbos afternoon. *Klal Yisrael,* he maintained, could not afford those few minutes of Reb Moshe's sleep.

He excelled in his personal attributes as much as he did in his scholarship. On one occasion when we were walking on the street on an *erev* Rosh Hashanah, a fellow approached the *Rosh Yeshiva* to beg his forgiveness for accusing him of being one who bears a grudge. Reb Moshe turned to the fellow and said: "You need not seek my forgiveness for I recite a prayer forgiving everyone who has wronged me or spoken ill about me."

As a rule the *Rosh Yeshiva* would never begin a conversation except where politeness dictated that he do so. He would always wait until he was spoken to before he would reply. He certainly did not have the time to relate stories as other, even distinguished, *rabbanim* commonly do.

Once at a wedding I was sitting next to him, at a table of other *rabbanim* and *baalei battim*. Naturally the *Rosh Yeshiva* was actively engaged in learning throughout the entire wedding until one of the *baalei battim* arose and demanded to know why the *Rosh Yeshiva* learns by himself when he is surrounded by so many other *rabbanim* and *roshei yeshiva*. Everyone present was aghast at the temerity of the man. Personally I wished to get up and pour a pitcher of water over his head, and my colleagues at the table were devising their own schemes.

But before we could execute any of our plans, the *Rosh Yeshiva* began to engage us in a discussion to calm the fellow's protest.

The Torah states, "And He called unto Moshe and the Lord spoke unto him out of the tent of meeting, saying..." (Vayikra 1:1). Rashi comments: before all instances of God speaking, and before all instances of 'saying,' and before all instances of 'commanding,' the term 'call' precedes, and this is a term of endearment." Rashi tells us (further on) that even as God was speaking to Moshe there were interruptions and disturbances.

God knows that upon occasion there should be disturbances in our learning. Reb Moshe, the Gaon who was always learning, had to talk to people, solicit funds, set up parlor meetings, travel out of town, etc. This too was the will of the Master of the Universe, except that for these interruptions God does not employ the term of endearment.

What was amazing was that when the *Rosh Yeshiva* did interrupt his learning to raise money, it was never for his own yeshiva. He would solicit for Chinuch Atzmai, or any other organization or institution that persuaded him that his help was needed.

And those who donated gave not because of their appreciation of the cause or the organization's work. They gave because of the *Rosh Yeshiva*. This was cruelly ironic, for the *Rosh Yeshiva* could not then return and collect from these same people for his own yeshiva. Yet these considerations did not trouble or daunt Reb Moshe. The people were donating to Torah, and Torah was his only concern.

The Talmud relates that one does not appreciate the words of his Rebbe until one reaches forty years of age. I understand this to mean that until the age of forty you think that you understand your Rebbe. However, once you turn forty, you realize that your Rebbe is so far above you that you *never* understood him.

For close to two years I escorted the *Rosh Yeshiva* every evening for long walks. At the time he was transcribing his *shiurim* on the second *perek* of Baba Kamma to appear in his *Dibros Moshe,* and he did not wish to publish them until he knew every *shiur* by heart.

The *Rosh Yeshiva* found me a fitting person with whom to discuss and to whom to relate the *shiurim;* I was, frankly, barely qualified. I was not knowledgeable in the *gemara,* let alone the *Rishonim.* There were several opportunities during the course of these walks that I managed to divert the subject to matters of importance to *Klal Yisrael* in which I was involved at the time.

Not being a keen observer, it took two years until I noticed that whenever I would speak to him on matters other than the *gemara* being analyzed, the *Rosh Yeshiva* would be moving his lips. He was learning while I was speaking to him, and still he managed to answer me!

Over two decades ago, there was a crisis on the East Side when the owner of the *mikveh* building threatened to sell it unless the religious community could raise what was at that time the astronomical sum of $25,000. The *Rosh Yeshiva* took charge and went from apartment to apartment to raise the money needed to preserve the *mikveh*.

I escorted the *Rosh Yeshiva* to an East Side shul the congregants of which were known to be very religious people. The *Rosh Yeshiva* had been invited to attend a board meeting there at which funds were to be allocated for the *mikveh*. For over an hour, however, a variety of other topics were discussed and the subject of the *mikveh* was left for last. When the matter was finally brought up, a collection was organized and a total of one hundred dollars was raised, a sum which clearly shamed the *Rosh Yeshiva*.

The *Rosh Yeshiva* commented that the prophet Ezekiel was called Yechezkael ben "Boozi," because he embarrassed himself, and Reb Moshe consoled himself with that thought.

It is our job, indeed our sacred obligation, to see to it that we award the proper honor and respect to our *Gedolim*. Furthermore, we must see to it that we cultivate in ourselves the sensitivity that our *Gedolim* have. Many people believe erroneously that the expertise of *Gedolim* is limited to *psak* and Talmud instruction.

Once during a *shiur* the *Rosh Yeshiva* quoted a *chiddush* that I had suggested. I nearly fainted when I heard my name mentioned, for who am I that he should quote me? However, Reb Moshe felt otherwise, because of his sensitivity. He could express his sensitivity at times when others would show restraint.

This point is well illustrated by students who raised questions in the middle of his *shiur*. Reb Aharon Kotler zt"l, for example, was reputed to be like a flaming torch when he would deliver his *shiur*. Interrupting Reb Aharon with a question in the middle of a *shiur* was nothing less than suicidal, and indeed those who had the temerity to ask, were known as "kamikazes."

Reb Moshe was no less disturbed by an interruption, for he put into his *shiurim* everything he had, yet he would patiently answer any question posed.

The high level of his *shiurim* I found awesome, and humbling. Yet when I would walk home from the *shiur* he would belittle his achievement and state that if you proceed on a smooth path you will arrive at the right thing.

When Elisha saw his Rebbe, Eliyahu, depart into the Heavens in a storm of wind and fire, he cried out: "My father, my father, the chariots of Yisrael and their horsemen!" (Melachim 2, 2:12). Such a verse is equally applicable to the passing of the *Rosh Yeshiva*. Although he had all of *Klal Yisrael* and all of their worries on his shoulders, he was like a father to each and every Jew. And in this way Reb Moshe emulated his Creator Who cares for the whole world and simultaneously tends to each and every creation.

When God came to visit the ailing Avraham *Avinu* who was recuperating from his *milah,* our Forefather rose to fetch guests who were wandering in the desert. From him we learn that hospitality and welcoming guests is more important than greeting even the Divine Presence. The question is: how did Avraham know this? How did he know that the mitzva of hospitality should be fulfilled not just by giving a paltry sum, but by taking into account the sensitivities of the guest.

The *Rosh Yeshiva* explained that the answer is implied in the Torah's phraseology. It says (Breishis 18:1): "And to him appeared the Lord" instead of, "And the Lord appeared to him." The operative word in this phrase is "to him." God abandoned all of his Heavenly activities and concerns to appear to man. He approached Avraham *Avinu* and inquired, "Avremeleh, how are you?" God did not appear in order to teach Torah but to demonstrate that care for a human being takes precedence over greeting the Divine Presence. This was Avraham's source, and a lesson which the *Rosh Yeshiva* embodied.

The *Rosh Yeshiva*'s dedication to learning defies description. Doctors advised that he suspend delivering his *shiur,* but Reb Moshe contended that it was beneficial for his *neshamah.* Instructions to eat more and sleep more also could not divert the *Rosh Yeshiva* from his schedule which devoted every minute to learning Torah. The Rebbetzen once commented to her husband that a page of *gemara* for him was like a glass of scotch for an alcoholic. Yet the *Rosh Yeshiva* would interrupt his study as soon as someone who wished to discuss something with him would enter the house.

Jews in Russia suffered terribly from the Communists. Most particularly the damage came from the Jewish Communists themselves, referred to as the *Yevsektsia*. They issued decree upon vile decree to limit the observance of Judaism and study of Torah. They demanded that all *Rabbanim* resign.

The *Rosh Yeshiva* ruled that it was a time of "*shmad*" and therefore one had to be prepared to lay down his life rather than violate the Torah's precepts. Those *Rabbanim* who capitulated and indeed resigned were sent to Siberia where many of them perished.

The Bolsheviks closed down the *mikveh* in Reb Moshe's town, yet he found a way of operating it clandestinely, albeit under conditions which were less than ideal halakhically, but still permissible. The *Rosh Yeshiva* did not himself rely on his own dispensation to use the *mikveh,* and separated himself from his wife for nearly six years. Once again we encounter the incredible self-sacrifice of the *Rosh Yeshiva:* for others he could rule leniently, easing their difficult existence; for himself he demanded strict observance regardless of the consequences.

Three areas where the *Rosh Yeshiva* especially excelled were in the realms of *Hasmada, Emunah,* and *Bitachon.* On one *achron shel Pesach* the *Rosh Yeshiva* appeared unusually disappointed. Reb Moshe had so earnestly believed that *Mashiach* would come that Pesach that he actually fretted over the realization that he had been wrong. Such was his belief in the *Mashiach.*

On another occasion his *bitachon* was illustrated when his son informed him that the doctors had given up hope for the life of a particular student. The *Rosh Yeshiva*'s immediate reaction was to state confidently that the boy would be all right.

The *Rosh Yeshiva* was also an "*ish shalom.*" He once accepted an invitation to deliver a *shiur* at a particular yeshiva, even though he was later severely criticized for having delivered a *shiur* there. Living in peace with fellow Jews, however, was more important to Reb Moshe than the criticism of hotheads.

Representatives of both the Mizrachi and the Agudah newspapers in *Eretz Yisrael* came to America at the same time to solicit funds for their newspapers since neither of them had sufficient subscribers. The *Rosh Yeshiva* disputed the need for two religious newspapers. "We all agree on Shabbos," he said, "on *Taharas HaMishpacha,* and on the need to spread Torah learning. And the news is all the same." Reb Moshe's attitude stemmed from his overwhelming desire for peace. Every disagreement, he felt, could be minimized for the sake of peace.

ובלע המות לנצח ומחה ה' אלוקים דמעה מעל כל פנים, אמן.

Thy Servant Moshe
Reb Moshe Feinstein

A Tithe in Time

I N THE EARLY 1940s, the first modern *mikve* in New York opened its doors to a grateful community. Constructed in a converted brownstone where East Broadway meets Grand Street on New York's famous Lower East Side, it replaced the dilapidated Ridge Street facility that was housed in a building adjacent to a livery stable. Cart horses and horse-drawn wagons were quartered at the stable, and visits to Ridge Street were accompanied by sights and sounds distinctly antithetical to the concepts of sanctity and purification which "*mikve*" embodies. The new facility, therefore, was a welcome addition to the thriving neighborhood.

Since before the turn of the century, the Lower East Side had been a haven for Jews from Eastern Europe. As world wars and civil strife devastated countries across the globe, more and more refugees flooded America's shores and many settled in the area closest to their port of entry. Family and friends from the "old country" awaited their arrival there and the infrastructure of a Jewish existence — including basic needs such as shuls, yeshivos and kosher food stores — was already firmly established. Three-

This chapter was written during Reb Moshe's lifetime.

quarters of all Jewish immigrants lived — at least for a time — on the Lower East Side, crowded into decrepit tenements along with Italian, Irish, Polish, Chinese and Russian refugees who found themselves in similarly impoverished circumstances. The Lower East Side teemed with humanity and bustled with commerce.

"My son, the doctor" is a phrase born on the streets of New York. It was there that the destitute Jews found employment of every description — from sewing lace handkerchiefs in the "sweat shops" of Center Street, to peddling rags and used clothing from push-carts — working fourteen to eighteen hours a day in order to send their sons to college. Only through secular education, they thought, could their children hope to rise above the squalor. Thus, the offspring of the greatest European talmudic scholars and the scions of noted chassidic dynasties evolved into a class of American professionals and businessmen. While many did not abandon religious practice in the process, the yeshiva and Torah study were no longer the focus of their activity.

BEFORE WORLD WAR II, several philanthropists poured huge sums of money into the renewal of the decaying slum neighborhood, erecting housing developments, parks and community centers, and the slum, if not eradicated, was at least pushed back and contained. Since the most urgent need was for decent housing, none of the religious institutions benefited from the philanthropy, and certainly not the old *mikve*. While it did not fall into disuse, the area in which it was located became more hazardous than ever. Anyone who ventured there after dark did so in peril for his life: the slum that had been pushed back ended on Ridge Street.

The construction of the new *mikve* was financed by a

long-term mortgage of $25,000, a veritable fortune at the
time, and the mortgager was a businessman who operated
the facility as a private enterprise for seventeen years. Its
new location made it both central to the sizable new housing
projects inhabited almost exclusively by Jews, and
accessible by pedestrian and vehicular traffic.

Its presence served to rejuvenate the neighborhood,
body and soul. Young families who would have relocated
uptown or to the suburbs, chose to remain on the Lower
East Side. The pleasant atmosphere and decor of the new
mikve and its convenient location encouraged countless
residents to avail themselves of the facility, including many
who had disdained and avoided the Ridge Street building.

In 1957, events took an unforeseen turn. Pete's House, an
adjunct of the Grand Street Settlement foundation for
underprivileged youth, set its sights on the *mikve* building,
the rear wall of which abutted its gymnasium. The directors
of the Grand Street Settlement viewed the *mikve* premises
as ideally suited for the expansion of the Pete's House gym
and approached the mortgage holder with an offer he could
not refuse. Word of the pending sale spread throughout the
community and reached Rabbi Moshe Feinstein, the *Rosh
Yeshiva* of Mesivta Tiferes Yerushalayim (M.T.J.).

HAVING RESIDED on the Lower East Side since his
emigration from Russia in 1936, HaGaon Reb Moshe
was a familiar figure on Grand Street, although few could
put a name to that distinguished face. Short in stature and
with a luxuriant white beard and lively, twinkling eyes, the
Rosh Yeshiva could often be seen in the company of his
learned sons and *talmidim,* striding majestically from his
Grand Street apartment to his rabbinical school at the far
end of East Broadway. Partly because of his great humility
and partly because of the preeminence of Reb Aharon

Kotler *zt"l*, Reb Moshe was not then a well-known personality outside of the tight Yeshiva circle. Nonetheless, he was a highly-respected Torah scholar and educator.

When Reb Moshe learned of the impending disaster, he realized that immediate and drastic action was called for. It did not require genius to predict what would happen to the level of observance in the neighborhood, and, ultimately, to the Jewish character of the community itself, if the *mikve* were to fall.

His initial approach to the mortgager met with failure; repeated appeals to the man's religious convictions and conscience fell on deaf ears. As a source of revenue, the facility had not turned out to be the "gold mine" the man had hoped it would, and the opportunity to unload it for a tidy sum was too tempting to pass up. There was no question of building another *mikve*: property values in New York had skyrocketed and the cost would have been prohibitive. The only hope, then, was to raise the funds to meet the price that Pete's House had offered and for the community itself to assume responsibility for the operation of the facility. This hope, however, was somewhat divorced from reality.

Thousands of Jews of every stripe called the Lower East Side their home but scattered as they were among a dozen apartment complexes and hundreds of *shtieblach*, any thought of uniting them behind a cause (the significance of which eluded many of them) constituted little more than a pipe dream. Never before had they amalgamated for any purpose — certainly not a religious one — and it was unlikely that any attempt to bring them together would meet with success. Reb Moshe, however, was not dismayed. The cause was too vital to be dismissed — so vital, in fact, that it took precedence over many of his myriad obligations.

In addition to the enormous responsibilities he bore as

Rosh Yeshiva of Mesivta Tiferes Yerushalayim, where he delivered a daily *daf shiur*, and personally examined all of the *smicha* candidates, every available moment of his time was accounted for by his personal learning schedule. He began his day at four in the morning and from then until he retired late at night, Reb Moshe was actively engaged in Torah study and in recording his *chiddushim* and *piskei halacha*. His telephone, always close at hand, rang incessantly with *klal Yisrael* on the line, and the *Rosh Yeshiva* had difficulty finding the time for the *dinei Torah* and occasional *gittin* which he hosted in his house every afternoon. Despite all this, he allocated countless hours to this project and proved to be a tireless campaigner when it came to a cause of such importance as the *mikve*.

RECOGNIZING THE NEED to conduct matters in a businesslike fashion, he called a meeting of local merchants and prominent businessmen and asked them to join him in this effort. Few could deny his impassioned appeal for their cooperation, but for a neighborhood that was, at best, lower-middle class, the sum of money required was beyond their limited means. Wealthy people did not live on the Lower East Side.

A committee to save the *mikve* was formed and like any wise board chairman or chief executive who surrounds himself with an advisory panel of experts, Reb Moshe chose some of the more successful business people as committee members. The *Rosh Yeshiva* himself sat at the helm. The task they had undertaken seemed overwhelming but Reb Moshe set an example that was impossible not to follow. At the end of exhausting work days, the committee members made time to attend frequent hours-long plenary meetings and campaign strategy sessions. The *Rosh Yeshiva* said,

"Just as we are enjoined to set aside a tithe of our income for charity, so are we obliged to allocate a tithe of our time and energy for our community." The committee did that — and more.

At the meetings, not a moment of awkwardness or discomfort passed for the committee members, several of whom were awed by the presence of the brilliant scholar. Reb Moshe always deferred to their greater commercial expertise and acumen, and treated them as equals, calling them "my esteemed friend" and "my honored colleague." No task — regardless of its triviality — was too demeaning, for the *Rosh Yeshiva* endowed the committee's endeavors with an aura of spirituality. Saving the *mikve* became a holy mission.

NOTICES WERE distributed to all the yeshivas and *shtieblach* and posted in stores and shops, followed by a door-to-door fund-raising effort. Night after night, fair weather or foul, these dignified committee members personally knocked on every door in the neighborhood, begging donations. Had every Jew on the Lower East Side been willing to contribute five dollars, enough money could have been raised to buy the *mikve and* Pete's House, and even put a down payment on the Grand Street Settlement to boot. But this was not meant to be.

A pathetic pile of bills and coins was dumped each week on the *Rosh Yeshiva's* desk and the committee members were losing heart. Their disappointment in their fellow residents knew no bounds. People who would have unhesitatingly purchased a box of *treife* Girl Scout cookies — only to throw it in the trash upon the little uniformed salesgirl's departure — dropped nickels and dimes into the *mikve*-solicitors' waiting hands, or closed the door in their faces. More extreme tactics were required.

Armed only with the force of his charismatic personality, Reb Moshe *himself* went out door-knocking. But his activities bore little more fruit than those of his "esteemed colleagues". Men of means rooted around in their pockets for loose change to hand to the illustrious "*meshulach*" and the *Rosh Yeshiva* learned on his own flesh the indignities his co-workers had suffered. His efforts, however, were not in vain.

The very fact that the *Rosh Yeshiva* would so demean himself for this cause served to drive home its salience, galvanizing the community at last, and the fund-raising campaign was given a much-needed boost. The campaign chest began to swell as contributions poured in, some from the most surprising quarters.

Encouraged by this development and by Reb Moshe's unswerving faith of optimism, the committee took a bold step. Since there was no possibility of raising the *entire* sum in time to meet the mortgage holder's deadline, they borrowed the remainder from "*Gemach*" funds and from private parties — and *personally* signed for the loans. If their fund-raising efforts were to fail, the committee members themselves would be burdened with awesome debts.

THREE YEARS after this holy mission was undertaken, the *mikve* mortgage was ceremoniously burned at a gala dinner and responsibility for operating the facility passed to the community at large. To this day, it stands in the heart of the Lower East Side, renovated, refurbished and ready to serve the flourishing neighborhood.

The moment Reb Moshe Feinstein shouldered the burden of saving the *mikve* he ceased to be "merely" a *Rosh*

Yeshiva and became instead a *Rosh Kehilla,* and the *kehilla* came first to know, and then to love and honor, the diminutive giant who dwelled in their midst.

An Ordinary Jew from New York

HOW DOES ONE become *Gadol HaDor* — the most highly-respected contemporary rabbinic authority? Is a competition of some sort staged, perhaps one judged by a council of Talmudic sages? Or does one — after meeting certain criteria — simply declare oneself a *gadol*? Can an ordinary Jew achieve such stature and universal acclaim? A *New York Times* [May 5, 1975] interviewer received the following reply from a gentleman who has often referred to himself as "an ordinary Jew from New York":

"Well, it begins with one person asking a question and receiving an answer he can live with, which is yet in perfect consonance with *halacha*. He tells his friends, I suppose, and they, too, bring their questions and they, too, receive viable, halachically sound answers. And so it goes. In time, one becomes accepted."

This "ordinary Jew from New York" has won international fame and adulation for his outstanding scholarship, brilliant insights and incisive commentaries. He has learned *Shas* over two hundred times and knows by heart all of the major commentaries on *Shulchan Aruch*;

has written seven impressive volumes of responsa as well as novellae on Talmud; and serves as *Rosh Yeshiva* of Mesivta Tiferes Yerushlayim and as member of the Council of Torah Sages of Agudath Israel of America. His vast achievements have earned him the respect of Jew and Gentile in every part of the civilized world.

But perhaps more than any Torah luminary in our generation, Rabbi Moshe Feinstein has won the heart of his people.

Had the interviewer asked the *Gaon* why he is so well-loved, Reb Moshe might have answered: "Perhaps it is because *I* love *them*." In word, deed, and thought, the *Rosh Yeshiva* has demonstrated countless times this deep, abiding affection and concern for his fellow man and for *Klal Yisrael* in particular.

REBBETZIN FEINSTEIN was very concerned. There was a wedding she had to attend, requiring that she be out of the house for several hours, and she disliked leaving the *Rosh Yeshiva* home alone. Reb Moshe refused to allow her to summon a relative or a student to stay with him and that meant no one would be around to screen his calls.

The Feinsteins' telephone was almost never silent. Calls routinely came in at every hour of the day and night from people seeking *piskei halacha,* advice on religious or personal matters, and assistance of every description; Reb Moshe responded to each one. He could never deny a caller his attention, despite his overcrowded schedule. The Rebbetzin, therefore, had taken to acting as his secretary, in an effort to insulate her husband to some degree from a demanding public.

Reb Moshe, she felt, was too kindhearted for his own good. He could not refuse anyone. Certainly, of the many calls he received, a majority were serious inquiries that required the *Rosh Yeshiva*'s intercession, but there was a significant number of nuisance callers who apparently carried the Feinsteins' telephone number in their pocket and had no compunctions about dialing it whenever the mood struck them.

The *Rosh Yeshiva*'s sensitive nature and his tremendous love for his people impelled him to devote time and energy even to the obviously deranged. How many hours he'd spent with these unfortunates over the years! she thought. And how many hours of precious sleep he'd forfeited to compensate for time lost from his studies and researches.

"I'm not going," she said at last.

"But you must!" the *Rosh Yeshiva* protested. "I'll be fine. Don't worry."

"How can you say you'll be fine when you know you can't turn anyone away? What if that unfortunate fellow phones — the one who called you a *gonnif* last week in front of the whole yeshiva, the one you invited to your office to chat for three-quarters of an hour?"

"Oh, you know about that. Well, he was truly a troubled person and needed help. Could I turn him away?"

"No, you could not. And that's just the point. Your concern for the well-being of others often causes you to disregard your *own* well-being."

"And that's as it should be. What's a few moments of my time when a fellow-Jew is crying out for help? A small sacrifice, that's all."

"Like that *almanah?*

"You mean that poor, distressed woman who stopped

me in the middle of the street to tell me her troubles? But it is a mitzva to support widows and orphans. So I offered her a ride — is that so much?"

"You offered her *your* ride," the Rebbetzin reminded her husband gently, "while you walked home in the rain."

"I needed some time to myself anyway. I had to review my lecture for the next day. Besides, I don't recall that it was raining, at least not very hard."

"And what about the perpetual houseguests who've been eating here regularly for more than a *decade?*"

"It's the least I could do! *Hachnasas orchim* is a very basic mitzva, as you know."

"Of course I know it is," the Rebbetzin said with a smile, "and I'm delighted to have guests share Shabbos with us. I'm not complaining you understand, but wouldn't you say that having a guest for five hundred and twenty-six consecutive *Shabbosim* is perhaps carrying a good thing just a bit too far? Never mind. I've decided not to go to the wedding."

"But you *must!*"

"I've made up my mind. If I leave you here alone, you'll be on the phone the whole time I'm away and then you'll be awake half the night catching up on your writing. And you'll probably get up extra early in the morning in addition to get back to your *paperlach.*"

"But they're expecting you."

She knew he was right — as usual. "I'll only go if you promise not to answer the phone."

"Alright," the *Rosh Yeshiva* agreed with a twinkle in his eye.

The Rebbetzin was still hesitant, but it was a family affair and, as Reb Moshe had pointed out, she had already notified her relatives that she would attend. Reluctantly, she consented to go, but only after Reb Moshe reiterated his assurance that he would not answer any calls.

S HE WAS NOT GONE five minutes when the telephone began to ring. Without even glancing up from his *sefer,* the *Rosh Yeshiva* stretched his hand out to lift the receiver. But there he stopped, suddenly remembering his promise to the Rebbetzin. He tried to ignore the ringing and return to his work, but it persisted for some time. He rose from his desk and went out of the room in order to put some distance between himself and temptation. The telephone bell, however, could be heard from every room of the Feinsteins' Lower East Side apartment.

"Perhaps it's an emergency, " he thought. "Some hapless Jew is suffering and needs solace. How can I deny him? Perhaps some neighborhood crisis has occurred, *chas v'shalom.* Surely the Rebbetzin will understand and forgive me." Only a few weeks earlier, the rabbi of a local shul had called in great distress. His shul had held a "Purim Carnival" for the youngsters and along with the various game booths, a "mock wedding" booth had been set up. To the rabbi's dismay, among the scores of children who had taken part in the "jest" were a dozen or more twelve- and thirteen-year-olds. Each boy had given a simulated gold ring to a girl and recited the *"Harei at."*

Their intention, of course, had been purely amusement and when the rabbi had become aware of what was transpiring in that booth, he had called an immediate halt to the festivities. Unless the *Rosh Yeshiva* knew of a *heter,* the "mock" *Kiddushin* were legitimate and binding; that is, the girls were, for all intents and purposes, married to the boys.

They would require a *get* to dissolve the marriage and would therefore be *grushos* — at the tender age of twelve! — and forbidden to *Cohanim.**

The report had been devastating. A foolish, childish prank had turned into a possible tragedy for perhaps a dozen neighborhood families. The ringing phone might *chalilah* be bringing word of a similar dilemma or of a catastrophe, one that could be prevented or mitigated by his intervention.

Reb Moshe hurried back to his desk and reached for the receiver. But just then, the phone stopped ringing. In a moment, he was again immersed in his work and his earlier concerns regarding the anonymous caller were forgotten.

BEFORE LONG, the telephone rang once more and once more his hand automatically moved to the receiver... and stopped." The Rebbetzin is right, of course," he told himself. "What would the caller do if I, too, had gone to the *chassanah?* He would solve his problem with the aid of some other rabbi, or come to my door in person, or call me later. I must pretend to myself that I'm not at home."

He knew that his Rebbetzin — like his children and other relations — had his best interests at heart. They tried to surround him with a protective shield to keep the possible "nudniks" at bay. During *Sukkos* one year, he recalled, at a relative's house in the suburbs, there had been a terrible commotion outside the *sukkah* and he'd asked his hosts repeatedly what the trouble was. His relatives had dismissed the ruckus as unimportant but when the *Rosh Yeshiva* had gone to the window to see for himself, a most astonishing sight appeared before his eyes. A group of *yidden* had literally been hanging from the branches of the

* The Torah forbids a *Cohain* to marry a divorcee. *Vayikra* 21:7

surrounding trees! Of course, he had greeted them — it was only right after the extremes they had gone to just to get a glimpse of him. The caller, too, might want nothing more than to hear a friendly voice, a kind word. How much time could that take from his work? Still, he had given the Rebbetzin his assurance.

T HE *ROSH YESHIVA* began to pace as he considered the problem and all the while the telephone rang persistently. "Perhaps it's an *agunah*," he thought, and his eyes filled with tears. There was no halachic solution for an actual *agunah* and each tragic case tore at his tender heart. "Or it may be one of those poor weak-minded individuals who are so put-upon by society, like that fellow who interrupted the *shiur* shouting 'Moishe! Moishe!' The boys wanted to throw him out, but I had him shown to my office. It only took an hour or so for him to calm down and I'm sure he felt better afterwards. I *must* answer. I know the Rebbetzin will understand."

But once more, the phone had stopped ringing by the time Reb Moshe reached for it and the *Rosh Yeshiva* returned to his labors. There was, as usual, a great deal of correspondence that required his attention and he was organizing the most recent *shailos* he'd received along with his *teshuvos* to be published as a new volume of *Igros Moshe*. In addition, he had to prepare his *daf shiur* and weekly *shiur klali*. It was fortunate that he had long ago accustomed himself to a barest minimum of sleep.

Then the phone rang for a third time.

He was unable to restrain himself. It might be the same desperate caller trying repeatedly to reach him. He grabbed the instrument. "Hallo?" he said.

A familiar voice came over the wire. "I thought we agreed that you were not to answer the phone!"

The Pious Patient

THE MOMENT Alice Murphy came on duty, she noticed that something had changed. She'd only been away for a week, yet the atmosphere in the hospital where she served as a "candy-striper" seemed different, less cold and antiseptic somehow and, well, friendly. She had waved to the switchboard operator when she'd entered the building and instead of the usual automatic return-wave, she'd received a brilliant smile in response.

Alice was about to ask, "To what do I owe this pleasure?" but the switchboard was flashing madly, and the operator only rolled her eyes skyward as she spoke into the headset. "Yes, thank God, his condition is stable... and God bless you too, sir. University Medical Center, good morning..." Alice hurried off to the bank of elevators.

One of Alice's responsibilities was the sorting and distribution of the patients' mail, a job that gave her enormous satisfaction because it enabled her to bring some joy to the infirm. But when she saw the huge pile of envelopes awaiting her attention, she was utterly confused. Had no one seen to the sorting in her absence? she wondered. A quick glance at the postmarks, however, revealed that the mail was all current. "What's going on here?" she asked a fellow volunteer.

"Why, nothing, Mrs. Murphy," the teenager replied. "The post delivery has been like that for days, but with God's help we've been able to manage even though we were shorthanded." That was twice in less than ten minutes she had heard the Deity's name invoked. Something peculiar was definitely afoot. Of that she was certain.

An intern wearing a *yarmulke* passed by her door and called, "Good morning, Mrs. Murphy. How was your vacation?"

"That does it!" she exclaimed. Although she was one of the few middle-aged "candy-stripers" at the hospital, her pink and white uniform had always cloaked her in invisibility. Rarely had any medical staff members so much as noticed her, let alone greeted her warmly. "Is something wrong with this place? Has everyone lost their marbles?"

"Not at all," the intern answered mildly. "Bless the Lord, everything is just fine."

Alice had a sneaking suspicion that "*He*" had checked in while she'd been away. Shrugging her shoulders, she bent to the task at hand, and soon it became apparent that the hospital was hosting a celebrity. Nearly a hundred cards, letters and telegrams were addressed to a single patient: Rabbi Moshe Feinstein. Arms piled high with mail, she strode off to see the "superstar" for herself.

WHEN SHE PUSHED open the door to his room, everything became clear. Propped up in bed like a monarch on his throne, the Rabbi was absorbed in a huge tome and surrounded by an almost palpable aura of spirituality. A snowy white beard spread down from his chin and a huge silk cap adorned his head, and when he glanced up from the text his face radiated such holiness as Alice Murphy had never seen before.

"And how are we feeling today, Rabbi?" she asked, trying to sound casual.

"*Baruch Hashem,*" Reb Moshe replied. His companion, a well-groomed young man, acted as translator. "Blessed be the Lord, I am well thank you. And yourself?"

Alice was awestruck. The patient clearly was *not* well: his room was crowded with medical apparatus and all of it was attached to him. Despite this, and unlike others who found themselves in similar circumstances, the Rabbi had voiced not a word of complaint but instead had inquired after *her* health. *And* his interest seemed genuine.

"I... I'm fine," she stammered.

"Please put down your burden," the Rabbi invited, noticing the load of mail she carried. "I'm so sorry to cause you such inconvenience."

"No, no, sir," she protested. "It's my pleasure!" She added her armload to the overflowing stack on the patient's nightstand and quietly withdrew. Even before she had reached the door, the Rabbi's face was buried again in the sacred volume. Alice Murphy knew she had been in the presence of greatness.

T HE *ROSH YESHIVA* had been brought to New York University Medical Center several weeks earlier in a very weak state, and the hospital had instantly been thrown into turmoil. With so many Jews on the staff who recognized the distinguished patient, the grapevine was soon humming with the news. From every department, noted physicians, whom the *Rosh Yeshiva* had consulted in the past on matters of *halacha*, flocked to his room to pay their respects, each deferentially donning a *yarmulke* before entering. Nurses vied for the privilege of attending him, and patients from every wing of the hospital gathered outside his room, hoping for a blessing for a *refu'ah sheleimah* or at least for a glimpse of the great man.

Each member of the staff who examined, served, tested, washed or injected the *Rosh Yeshiva* was rewarded with his gratitude, his blessing and his apology for the inconvenience. Each left his room wearing a dazed, glowing expression. The dietician who brought his breakfast was asked if she herself had eaten something nourishing that morning. The male nurse who dozed fitfully at Reb Moshe's bedside was offered a suggestion for a more practical arrangement of the chairs that would enable him to sleep more comfortably. And a certain lab technician learned the meaning of "*bitachon*."

When the technician from Hematology came to draw a specimen of Reb Moshe's blood, her hands were trembling with trepidation. Skill and experience notwithstanding, drawing blood samples from geriatric patients is always a complicated procedure because of the presence of numerous weakened or collapsed veins. Locating a functional one on the first try is a veritable impossibility.

Although she prided herself on the almost painless technique she had perfected, the lab technician was sure that drawing this specimen would require several punctures. In addition to her own reluctance to cause further discomfort to an ailing patient, she was certain that to do so with this *particular* patient would elicit a severe reprimand from the attending physician, a tongue-lashing from the hematology resident and, quite possibly, a lecture from the hospital administrator.

As she approached his bed with tourniquet and hypodermic in hand, the *Rosh Yeshiva* looked up from his studies and confidently presented his arm. "It's alright," his eyes reassured her. Yet she hesitated. He gave her an encouraging smile as if to say "God will guide your hand. Have faith." She plunged the needle into his frail arm and watched in amazement as the syringe rapidly filled with bright red blood.

B Y THE SEVENTH of Adar, which was Reb Moshe's ninetieth birthday — and not incidentally, that of Moshe *Rabeinu*, for whom he was named — the *Rosh Yeshiva's* condition had improved. Several of his relatives thoughtfully provided elaborately decorated cakes and tortes to mark the occasion. This day was not to pass unnoticed in New York University Medical Center — a vast hospital complex, occupying three square city blocks of midtown Manhattan, with hundreds of medical, technical, administrative and maintenance employees on its staff and a commensurate number of patients in its various wards.

The *Rosh Yeshiva*, whose restricted diet proscribes the consumption of foods with a high sugar content, could not allow the beautiful birthday confections to go to waste. In his halting English, he asked a patient from a nearby ward: "You vant some cake?"

Word went out that the Rabbi was dispensing birthday cake, and New York University Medical Center, staff and patients, lined up to wish Reb Moshe a "Happy Birthday" and receive their piece of the pie. It became a matter of pride and honor to be among the recipients of the portions which the pious patient graciously distributed, as these, rumor had it, had been blessed by the great man himself.

THE BUZZER sounded repeatedly at the nurses' station, and the lighted board blinked with urgency. It was room 1201: Mr. Hearst. The duty nurse did not interrupt her phone conversation, but eyebrow-signalled an aide to respond to the buzzer, and the girl hurried off down the corridor.

"When I want a *student* nurse," the irate patient fumed, "I'll *ask* for one. How long must a person ring in order to get some help around here?" William Randolph Hearst was unaccustomed to indifferent treatment.

"I'm sorry, sir, but everyone else is busy right now. There's an important patient on the floor."

"Well look around you, honey," Hearst instructed, implying that if there was anyone important at N.Y.U. Medical Center, it was William Randolph Hearst. "You think Medicaid paid for this suite?"

"No, no, of course not," the flustered girl replied. "I didn't mean..."

"Yeah, yeah. Forget it. Who is this big shot, anyway?"

"It's Rabbi Feinstein!" she whispered reverently.

"Who?" he demanded. Hearst was almost fully recovered from his illness and had reached the cantankerous stage. He was aware that his behavior was abominable, but orneriness, he felt, was the privilege of the affluent and influential.

"Rabbi Moses Feinstein," the student nurse explained, "the great rabbinic authority."

"Well, get him *in* here, girl. I'll give him a double-spread feature in one of my magazines. Tell him I'll make him famous."

The nurse dissolved in a fit of helpless giggling. Needless to say, the *Rosh Yeshiva* declined the offer.

TWO RELIGIOUS residents sat in the hospital cafeteria comparing notes on their illustrious patient. "When I did my internship at St. Vincent's Hospital, Reb Moshe was there," the first related, "and when they told him he'd need surgery to implant a pacemaker, he really got upset. I don't think I've ever seen him so distressed."

"It's not surprising," his colleague said. "Surgery can be a rather terrifying experience — especially for older people."

"Oh, he wasn't worried about the operation. He said that when the Redemption comes, he might be unable to fulfill his duty should the Messiah call upon him to serve in the *Sanhedrin*. The implant could render him a *baal mum* — legally 'blemished' — thereby disqualifying him for service in the *Sanhedrin*."

WHEN REB MOSHE learned that Senator Jacob Javits, who suffers from Lou Gehrig's Disease, had been admitted to the Medical Center, he immediately closed the volume in his lap. Over the vehement protests of his nurse, he climbed down from the hospital bed and into a wheelchair.

"What's the matter?" the male nurse cried in dismay. "Where are you going?"

"A Jew such as he, who has done so much for *Klal Yisrael,* is in the hospital — I must be *mevaker choleh*." And with that, the *Rosh Yeshiva* began to wheel himself out of the room.

It is said that a man's true character is revealed in three areas: his finances, his flask, and his fury. When it comes to money matters, when he is "in his cups," and when he loses his temper, a man's rein on his natural impulses snaps and the opaque shield behind which he conceals his inner self becomes transparent.

There is, however, one more state wherein man is stripped of his defenses: his infirmity. Can a fevered brain control the words that escape slack lips? Can debilitated flesh be made to respond to the commands of the soul? The answer, obviously, is yes — when the soul has so saintly a master as Reb Moshe.

Give Truth to Yaakov
Reb Yaakov Kamenetsky

To Bruck
Or Not To Bruck

THERE ARE three ways to identify a Litvak: the Slow Way, the Quick Way, and the Sure Way.

According to the "Slow Way," one must first strike up an acquaintance, and get to know the person. The Litvak will soon reveal his incisive, analytical bent of mind — an attribute on which he prides himself. Likewise, with time, one may discern a slight aloofness of nature.

The "Quick Way" — more direct — is by simply listening to his pronunciation, e.g.: "Torah" in Galician dialect is *Toy-ruh*, whereas in Lithuanian dialect it is *Tay-reh*. "Fish un Fleish" becomes *Fiss un Fleiss*. There is evidence as well in his liturgy: does he say *Hodu* or *Baruch Sheamar*? Does he say *Kegavna* or *Ba'me Madlikin*?

It should be borne in mind, though, that the above methods are inconclusive. The one "Sure Way" of identifying a Litvak is by observing his custom on Passover: a Litvak worthy of the name eats *gebrochts*.* It's practically

---

* Because of uncertainty if all the flour in a matza is thoroughly baked, some refrain from allowing matza to come in contact with water, which might cause the unbaked flour to leaven. Such moistened matza is referred to as "gebrochts."

This chapter was written during Reb Yaakov's lifetime.

a matter of principle. Any Litvak who does *not* eat *gebrochts* is clearly an imposter.

I T IS ALL the more perplexing, then, that Reb Yaakov Kamenetsky, the *gaon* of Lithuanian Jewry, abstains from this tradition of his fellow countrymen, even on the last day of *Pesach*, when many chassidim are inclined to indulge. The explanation has nothing to do with genealogy but rather with Reb Yaakov's conception of honesty.

As a young teenager, Reb Yaakov, like the other yeshiva *bochurim* in Slobodka, ate *teg* — "daily" meals at the homes of various *baalei batim*. The students in almost every case were dependent upon the generosity of these householders for sustenance and could therefore ill afford to be too selective.

O NE PASSOVER, Reb Yaakov received an invitation to a home where the standard of kashrus was questionable. When he realized that the alternatives he was faced with were either to partake of a possibly "*treifa*" meal or to embarrass his hosts by refusing a gracious invitation, Reb Yaakov saw but one solution to his predicament: He informed his host that, to his profound regret, it was not his custom to eat *gebrochts* during *Pesach*.

So that this statement, entirely legitimate within the framework of "the ways of peace," should not be construed as a falsehood, Reb Yaakov resolved from that moment on never to eat *gebrochts*.

The Truth Hurts

ONE EARLY MORNING on his way to *cheder*, Yaakov Kamenetsky was detained by a distraught young man. "*Yingeleh*," the man pleaded, "I know you're on your way to *daven* and learn Torah, but I am in desperate need of help." The man was so distressed that Yaakov would gladly have performed any deed in order to help. As it was, the man's request was but a simple one:

"My son's bris is scheduled to take place momentarily and in my nervousness and haste I neglected to bring the baby's blanket. My guests have already arrived and it would be improper for me to leave them in order to return home now. Please, *yingeleh*, be so kind as to do this great *chessed* for me." He pressed a key into Yaakov's small hand. "My house is on Pilsudskiego Street, Number 3, and the blanket is on the kitchen table."

Happy to oblige, six-year-old Yaakov Kamenetsky accepted the key and hurried to Pilsudskiego. He made his way quickly through the narrow, winding streets of the shtetl, looking neither left nor right, intent only on the performance of the mitzva.

AT LAST, mission accomplished, he once again set off for school, but his detour caused him to arrive at *cheder* twenty minutes late. A stern-faced *rebbe* greeted him at the door.

"Where have you been all this time?" the *rebbe* demanded. Yaakov explained the delay and apologized for his tardiness.

His *rebbe*, however, was skeptical. He was convinced that Yaakov had stopped on the way to *cheder* to watch the construction work going on at a nearby building site — a temptation few of his classmates were able to resist. Angry at the child for inventing an excuse, the *rebbe* slapped Yaakov across the face!

Reb Yaakov found it difficult, even many years later, to condone his *rebbe*'s behavior. "It is essential for a *rebbe* to know his students well enough to be able to determine when — and if — they are lying. Punishing a child when he tells the truth is unforgivable..."

Post Paid

THE POSTAL SERVICE in Tzitivyan, Lithuania was computerized long before the high-tech age of automated banks and electronic cash registers: it had Valinkov. Valinkov's brain was like a pocket calculator. He could add up a column of figures standing on his head and never make a mistake. Indeed, so accustomed were the townspeople to his unerring accuracy that they never even bothered to count their change.

Except once. On that fateful day Valinkov had had an argument with his wife and a Jewish customer benefited from the clerk's distraction. By chance he counted his change and discovered, to his amazement, that an error had been made in his favor.

He returned at once to the post office and said humbly to the clerk: "I'm afraid, sir, that your arithmetic was wrong."

Valinkov was irate, offended by the affront to his impeccable reputation, and quickly whipped out a fresh sheet of scrap paper to redo his calculations.

But no matter which way he added, the total differed from his original one. "You see?" the Jew said, "I was given fifteen kopecks extra," and he placed a handful of coins on the counter and left.

T HE CLERK was speechless. *No one* — least of all a Jew — reimbursed the Government! Why, in those years (between the World Wars) Lithuania's Jewish population was sufficiently victimized by governmental agencies to justify grand larceny. But this? This insignificant overpayment didn't even qualify as pilfering; it was more like a gift, albeit a modest one. And who would reject a gift from the Government?

"Perhaps," thought the clerk, "that is the reason he returned the money — it was too paltry a sum to be worth the risk of being caught." Valinkov decided to test the next Jew who entered the post office, this time with a more irresistible amount. True, he would have to make up the deficit from his own pocket, but it was worth it.

Later that day, Valinkov went ahead with his plan. When the Jew discovered the discrepancy, he was tempted to remain silent and simply enjoy the Government's unexpected largesse. His conscience, however, gave him no rest. He brought his dilemma before Tzivityan's rabbi — Reb Yaakov Kamenetsky.

Reb Yaakov made his *psak* perfectly clear: a Jew is forbidden to possess even the smallest fraction of a coin that does not rightfully belong to him. Word spread swiftly throughout the town.

It was just before closing time and Valinkov had been congratulating himself on his perspicacity when the Jew walked into the post office. The bewildered clerk could do nothing but accept the proffered bundle of notes. "Can they all be so naive... or honest?" he wondered.

Again and again the clerk tested the honesty of the Jews of Tzivityan, but Reb Yaakov's firm ruling and his sterling example fortified the people and they withstood the trials.

WHEN THE Nazis marched into Tzivityan one year later, it was this Gentile clerk, and this Gentile alone, who risked his own safety to rescue the Jews of the town. They had proven themselves to be a holy people, undeserving of such a dire fate.

The Scholarly Seer
Reb Yaakov Yisrael Kanievsky

The Scholarly Seer

O
N A SNOWY WINTER evening, a student from the Novardhok yeshiva was assigned to sentry duty. Like all of the other Jewish men conscripted into the Russian army, he had no alternative but to obey orders, regardless of any personal objections or religious conflicts this entailed. And this Friday night was no exception.

The sub-zero temperatures of the Russian winter dictate the attire required for outdoor activity, but a proper overcoat was beyond the means of the young yeshiva *bochur*. He asked the guard whom he was to relieve for the loan of his warm coat at the end of the guard's shift. It was not at all uncommon for soldiers to share equipment or clothing and the guard was happy to oblige. However, when he was ready to go off duty, he saw that his replacement was deeply engrossed in learning by heart and so, rather than disturb the young student, he hung the bulky army coat on a nearby tree and left.

For a while, the yeshiva student, cloaked in the warmth of his learning fervor, remained oblivious to the cold. But a sudden frigid gust of wind interrupted his concentration, and he became aware of the numbness in his extremities and the chill at his back. He was surprised to find himself manning the post alone, and dismayed to discover that the coat, so kindly left for him by his predecessor, hung tantalizingly from the outstretched branch of a nearby tree.

There was no doubt that the weather posed a very real risk to his life, a condition which entitled him to violate the rabbinic prohibition of removing something from a tree on the Sabbath. Nonetheless, he decided with the fullest conviction that his life was not yet in peril. — "... I shall wait another two minutes before I transgress the rabbinic ordinance in order to protect my health." And so he passed the entire Friday night in sub-zero weather, waiting and debating: "Another two minutes... Just two more minutes," until he was relieved by the next guard. Thus was the young Jewish soldier spared from violating the holy Sabbath.

THIS SOLDIER'S NAME was Yaakov Yisrael Kaniev-sky. He came to be known and revered by all as "the Steipler" (for Hornosteiple, the Ukrainian town of his youth). And when he passed away some 65 years after his Red Army service, more than two hundred thousand Jews accompanied this great Torah leader to his final resting place. That incident in the Russian winter paved the path of unrivalled greatness which he was to follow. A life composed of "Another two minutes, just two more minutes" of learning and disseminating Torah resulted in the Steipler's becoming a legend in his own lifetime.

The Steipler possessed what many considered to be *ruach haKodesh,* an ability to see beyond the visible, to penetrate suppressed thoughts and hidden motives. Furthermore, it was believed that his saintliness placed him on a plane above mortal man, a level from which the lines of communication with the Almighty were more direct. The Steipler's private advice and blessings, therefore, were sought by hundreds of Jews each day. Jews of every stripe made the pilgrimage, some travelling great distances and across oceans to reach his house in Bnei Brak, and hear the *Tzaddik's* words.

He lived simply, in a small room, with cracked floor tiles and peeling plaster, a plain wooden table and chairs, and hundreds, perhaps thousands, of *sefarim*. It was to that humble house on Rashbam Street in Bnei Brak that hundreds of troubled Jews flocked daily, waiting hours for a moment in his presence, to seek knowledge, advice, counsel or blessing.

Because his hearing was severely impaired the Steipler had to receive all requests in writing. But this in no way detracted from his fulfillment of the role for which he had been destined. His was the broad shoulder upon which countless sufferers cried. He comforted, consoled and instructed *Klal Yisrael* regarding problems of every description. His heart was big enough to accommodate every Jew.

During the course of a normal workday, a busy physician might see twenty or thirty patients, at most. The Steipler received ten times that number and the orderly progression of those who wished to enter was a result of *derech eretz,* and not the managerial skill of an efficient secretary. Each visitor would find the Gaon in precisely the same pose: bent over a *sefer,* intent on its contents. Thus he wasted not a moment from learning, glancing away from the text only when his undivided attention was required. Frequently he would snatch a few seconds of learning between one query and the next from the very same person.

On the previous page:
Slichos *in the Lederman Shul*
near the Steipler's home on Rashbam Street in Bnei Brak.
Below and facing page: his last shiur
(delivered on the occasion of the yahrzeit
of his brother-in-law, the Chazon Ish,
in Kollel Chazon Ish, *Bnei Brak).*

YAAKOV YISRAEL KANIEVSKY was born on the second of *Tammuz* 5659, and orphaned from his father at the age of seven. Despite so tragic a loss at so tender an age, he became an avid, intelligent pupil. When he was nine years old, a recruiter for the famed Novardhok Yeshiva network discovered the amazingly astute youngster, and brought him into Novardhok's main branch located in the town of Homel. It was the beginning of a brilliant learning career for the boy who was to become the revered Steipler Rav.

The young student made swift and astounding progress at Novardhok, but his education was interrupted by his conscription into the Russian army. Nevertheless, the Steipler's learning continued uninterrupted. During his entire time in the army — living under very difficult conditions among hosts of Gentiles, including numerous virulent anti-Semites — he did not diminish his study or compromise his strict observance of the mitzvos.

Soldier Kanievsky had reason to suspect that the heavy army-issue winter uniforms contained *shaatnez,* and he therefore refused to don the compulsory outfit. He lodged his complaint in writing to the army officials, saying that his religion prohibited the wearing of certain fabrics. His letter was forwarded up through the ranks, from his commanding officer to the officer's superior, and then on to even *his* superior. No one knew how to respond to this unusual complaint! Eventually, his protest landed on the desk of none other than the Secretary General of the Communist

Party, who summarily dismissed the problem by saying, "Let the Jew wear whatever he wants..."

The Czar's directive quickly reached the Steipler's base, and he was promptly admitted into a clothing warehouse and allowed to choose whichever uniform he wished. After inspecting the array of outfits, he selected a lightweight summer uniform — entirely inappropriate for the local climate, but the only outfit which allayed the Steipler's fear of wearing *shaatnez*.

WHILE SERVING in the Red Army, the Steipler was forced to participate in training and maneuvers which were held daily, including Saturday. Soldier Kanievsky, however, was determined not to violate Torah law by firing a gun on the holy Sabbath. His solution to this problem was to hold his weapon upside down with the trigger pointed upward, thereby transgressing the law only in an unconventional way and avoiding a Torah prohibition. To the astonishment of all, the Steipler succeeded in striking targets accurately with his reverse firing — an achievement which caused a sensation in the local press.

On one such occasion, when obeying orders would have entailed a flagrant violation of Torah law, he refused to comply. As penalty for insubordination, he was forced to run the gauntlet, a punishment which he actually treasured for it was precipitated by his observance of the mitzvos.

The Steipler managed to be released from the army in a relatively short period of time, and he returned to the Novardhok yeshiva. In 5682, however, most of the Novardhoker students in Russia were smuggled across the border into Poland. There, the Steipler entered the "Bais Yosef" Novardhok yeshiva in Bialystock, which was under the direction of the *Sabba fun Novardhok*'s son-in-law, Rabbi Avraham Yaffen.

RABBI YAFFEN WAS AMAZED by the Steipler's diligence. He once related to his students, "Reb Yaakov Yisrael used to eat in my house every Shabbos, and of course his head was always in a *sefer* for the duration of the meal. One time, all of the guests had finished eating and *benching* while the Steipler, absorbed in his study, remained unaware of the meal's conclusion. My wife, who had recently given birth to a girl, wished to show the yeshiva students how great a *masmid* the Steipler was. She gathered everyone's attention and then turned towards the Steipler, who was still engrossed in his study, and asked, 'Reb Yaakov Yisrael, why didn't you, such a close friend, attend our son's *bris?*' The Steipler answered lamely that he hadn't had the time, and resumed his study. 'You see,' she said to all who were present, 'the child that was born to me was a girl and the entire yeshiva, indeed the whole town, has been talking about it, but Reb Yaakov Yisrael is none the wiser.' "

Reb Yaakov Yisrael's diligence was indeed phenomenal. Once, on his way into the *beis midrash,* he overheard two students discussing a possible problem of *shaatnez* commonly found in certain jackets. Not wishing to waste any time from learning to investigate the matter, he ripped out the lining of his jacket, and promptly sat down to learn.

While he was in Bialystock, the Steipler wrote a volume of talmudic novellae entitled *Shaarei Tevunah,* a book which brought him immediate fame in the yeshiva world. When the book reached the hands of the Chazon Ish, one of the very greatest scholars of the period, he inquired about the author. Upon discovering that it had been written by a young unmarried student, he immediately suggested a match between his sister, Miriam, and the author. It was not long after that the couple were wed in a ceremony attended by the older *bochurim* from all the yeshivos in the area. (The Chazon Ish's only regret regarding the match was that the idea had come to him in the middle of the *shemoneh esrei.*)

After his marriage, Reb Yaakov Yisrael became a *Rosh Yeshiva* in the "Bais Yosef" yeshiva in Pinsk. He had been teaching in the yeshiva for six years when word arrived from his brother-in-law, the Chazon Ish, who had settled in *Eretz Yisrael.* The Chazon Ish said that he would like them to join him in the Holy Land, and the Steipler, as always, faithfully fulfilled his brother-in-law's request without any hesitation. (His fidelity and deference to the Chazon Ish is exemplified by a statement he once made, "Whatever the Chazon Ish did not forbid is permitted, and what he did not permit is forbidden.") Directly after the Purim *Seudah* in 5692, the Steipler left Pinsk for the Holy Land, where he became the *Rosh Yeshiva* of "Bais Yosef"-Novardhok in Givat Rokeach in Bnei Brak, a position which he held for over 25 years.

THE YESHIVA the Steipler headed eventually closed due to serious financial problems, and he was compelled to turn to the other local yeshivos for meals. He and his wife cared for the aging Chazon Ish, whose rented apartment they shared until his passing. On the day after the *shiva* of the Chazon Ish, the Steipler learned that the landlord wanted to nullify the lease for fear that the Kanievskys might try to inherit the apartment. As soon as the Steipler heard this rumor, he moved all that he owned out of the house and onto the street, although he had nowhere to go.

Kollel Chazon Ish, of which he had become the head with his brother-in-law's passing, provided him with an apartment on Rechov Rashbam in Bnei Brak, and spared his having to spend the night under the stars. When the owner of the Chazon Ish's apartment later discovered who the

Steipler was, he was filled with remorse and came to the Steipler frequently to make sure that he had secured his forgiveness.

The passing of the Chazon Ish forced the Steipler to enter the limelight — under duress, to be sure. His counsel was sought on all matters of urgency. But far more important in establishing the Steipler as an unparalleled Gaon — far more important than even his brilliant advice — was his work: the *Kehillos Yaakov.*

A series of books which rivals the Chafetz Chaim's *Mishna Brurah* in popularity, the *Kehillos Yaakov* can be found in virtually every yeshiva and in countless homes. Masterpieces of lucidity, they are the barometer by which one determines if one has truly mastered a Talmudic subject — for all of the trenchant points in the Talmud are discussed therein. There is no other scholarly work on *shas* so easily comprehensible. Writing in such a readily understandable style was a challenge which the Steipler conceded was often more difficult than the novellae themselves.

IN ADDITION TO his contribution to Torah scholarship, the Steipler was noted for his private advice and blessings, sought by hundreds of Jews on a daily basis. The Steipler offered his advice in such a simple, straightforward way that some imagined that he was addressing another supplicant, or that he had not grasped the problem. But, clearly, the Steipler, whose wisdom and perceptiveness were unchallenged, understood. Psychologists who were subsequently consulted about the very same problems were amazed by the Steipler's perspicacity and keen understanding of the human psyche.

Requests for advice or a blessing were subject to several

stipulations: first, the request had to be in writing, as the Steipler was hard of hearing; and second, the supplicant had to be a Torah observer, as the Steipler objected to helping someone who was bent on using his blessing to perpetuate iniquitous ways.

Once a fellow in dire financial straits went to the Steipler for a blessing, but the moment he entered the Steipler reprimanded him severely for not wearing *tzitzis* and denied him an audience. Terribly shaken, the fellow ran to the Steipler's grandson and asked, "What can I do now? I am so unnerved by your grandfather's berating. How could he have known I wasn't wearing *tzitzis?* What shall I do?"

"The first thing you should do," came the response, "is put on a pair of *tzitzis* and then go back to him."

The fellow was aghast. "How dare I return? He will certainly recognize me for I was there only today." But the Steipler's grandson insisted. "Do as I say, and see what happens."

The fellow put on a pair of *tzitzis* and went back to the Steipler. This time the Steipler calmly received him, without any reference to the morning's encounter, and blessed him with success.

A THIRD STIPULATION, adopted later on, was that the Steipler would neither receive women nor read requests penned by them.

In the course of a day, dozens, sometimes hundreds of requests accumulated from people who were unable to get in to see the Steipler. He would read through each and every one of the requests late at night, with even more attention than he allocated to the requests of those who saw him in person. "Those who met with me, I was able at least to comfort partially," he reasoned, "while these requests belong to people who were unable to wait or were turned away."

He would unfold and read the requests one by one, but several he would discard without even opening. "These were written by women," he explained to the utter astonishment of those whose investigation confirmed the accuracy of his claim.

The last stipulation was that he did not allow requests to be written on *Chol Hamoed* (with the exception of a supplication for one who was ill), a practice which incidentally provided the Steipler a two-week vacation each year from bearing the yoke of the Jewish people. [A fellow once met the Steipler in a shul during *Chol Hamoed* and was very anxious to receive the latter's blessing. But what could he do? The Steipler, as was well known, would not allow requests to be written to him during the holiday. He suddenly thought of an idea. He ran over to the wall and removed a sign which he displayed in front of the Steipler's eyes. It read: *vesain bracha.*]

Countless visitors came to write their requests over the years, leaving behind more than 1000 abandoned writing implements of every description, all of which he saved in a special box *ad sheyavo Eliahu.* But the quantity of pens and pencils, markers and crayons is outnumbered by the countless stories of the Steipler's sagacity, wit, clairvoyance — and outright miracles.

The Steipler's usually terse responses often seemed only partially related to the question posed. Sometimes the Steipler would be deliberately ambiguous or noncommittal — and that would be his answer.

A MAN ONCE CAME to the Steipler, allegedly seeking counsel about whether to sell his apartment for a very fair price to the Ministry of Welfare. He would be able to make a handsome profit, but the neighbors were opposed. The Steipler's response was, "You know better than I," and would say no more.

He later explained to a family member that the person posing the question had not been truly interested in an answer. What he had sought was a quote from 'the Steipler' vindicating his sale, which he would have been able to use against angry neighbors. "Since this was the case, my only answer to him could be 'you know better than I' — I would not provide him with the excuse he wanted."

To fathers seeking matches for their daughters, he recommended that they look for the following three characteristics in the boy: diligence, a clever mind, and good attributes. "Certainly a diligent Torah student must be one who possesses good attributes?" he was asked.

The Steipler disagreed. "To be a *masmid* means to have learned six years in yeshiva with *gemara* and *shtender*. But these two items place no demands upon a person. A *shtender* has yet to ask for assistance, for the trash to be taken out, that some errands be run, and so on. A *shtender* has never shown a disagreeable face to a *masmid* or asked him for some words and gestures of consolation and encouragement. Nor has a *gemara* ever taken ill and required care... And all of a sudden the *masmid* must begin a life together with a woman who may demand all of the above and far more! Good attributes, therefore, are essential in addition to diligence..."

The Steipler displayed little patience for older bachelors who were bitter over not having found their mate. He maintained that each had indeed met his mate, but had rejected her. "God does not force you to wed. As long as you are looking for *bedavka* — she must have exactly this, and this, and that — you will never accept the wife who was meant for you. Far better for you to be less particular now, and work more on achieving compatibility and *shalom bayis* once you are wed."

On the previous page:
the man the Steipler respected the most,
HaRav Eliezer Menachem Shach.
To the right: the last picture taken
(moments after the completion of a Sefer Torah).
Facing page: leaving nichum aveilim at the Karelitz family:
the Steipler with יבל"ח (counterclockwise from upper right)
Dr. Rothschild, his son (featured on the following page)
Reb Chaim, and his son Avraham Yishayahu Kanievsky.

IT WAS NOT UNCOMMON for petitioners to listen very carefully to the way in which the Steipler would read aloud the handwritten notes presented to him. The slightest pause, gesture or editing of the request might indicate a partial response, or shed light on some mysterious element. Often his Divine Inspiration was thus revealed.

In the beginning of Operation Peace for Galilee, two newly-observant Israeli combat pilots came to the Steipler with an urgent, indeed secret, request. They had already been briefed concerning the mission they were to undertake the following day: the destruction of the as yet invincible Russian-made SAM 6 anti-aircraft missile batteries in the Bekaa Valley, deep in enemy territory. Reconnaissance flights indicated that the missile pads were heavily defended and Intelligence revealed that they were manned by Soviet technicians and personnel.

The ultra-sophisticated SAM 6s would be automatically activated the moment enemy aircraft entered a twenty kilometer radius of the launch pads. At an amazingly great distance, these missiles are able to lock onto the heat-producing elements of their targets and follow even an evasive course at speeds exceeding Mach 1.

All of the usual techniques employed so effectively by the Israel Air Force to evade radar detection — such as flying at low altitudes, the jettisoning of heat balloons and showers of metallic fragments, tactics which confounded standard radar equipment — would be useless against the advanced technology of the SAM 6s. It would take more than the usual combination of raw courage, combat excellence and precise coordination to turn the odds in the IAF's favor. An extra measure of *Siyatta de'Shmaya* was definitely called for.

The Steipler read the pilots' request, which indicated that the mission was scheduled for 0800 the next morning. He gave them his blessing and said he would begin saying *Tehillim* for them at seven o'clock. The pilots tried to indicate through hand signals that take-off was scheduled for eight a.m., not seven. But the Steipler disregarded their protests. He repeated, this time emphatically, that he would recite *Tehillim* at seven o'clock.

Shortly before dawn, Israeli intelligence provided additional data and the high command issued a directive advancing the mission by one hour. The IAF fighter squadron returned safely to base at 0723 — Mission Accomplished.

THE STEIPLER would not allow the daily accumulation of written requests to be removed from his table until he had recited a chapter from *Tehillim* over all of them, as was his custom before retiring. The slips were then placed in a bag, eventually to be buried.

The plight and suffering of others was his primary concern; he paid little or no attention to his own needs. His lifestyle was the epitome of simplicity, lacking any hint of embellishment. The meagerness of his quarters — a sheetless mattress on a narrow iron cot, no pillow or any other comfort or luxury — typified the humility of the man.

He laughed and cried without inhibition. In the most ordinary and unassuming way, he made extraordinary predictions and performed miraculous deeds, with neither fanfare nor flourish. His hearing impairment caused him to *daven* out loud, unaware that bystanders could hear his fervent outpouring of emotion.

The Steipler's humbleness and abnegation made him refuse to be driven to shul in the morning despite his great difficulty in walking. Once a devoted follower laid in ambush for the Steipler, waiting with a car outside his door. After this happened two days in a row, the Steipler arose especially early, rushing out the door alone, for fear that the driver, whom he had begged not to come, might be waiting for him again.

One Friday night, the Steipler suddenly appeared at the home of a young married man. The student who had accompanied the Steipler on the long walk explained that on that very day this *avrech* had visited the Steipler to ask him to pray for his ailing wife. Upon reflection, the Steipler had become concerned that he might not have provided enough encouragement for the *avrech* and he had not been able to rest until he had reassured the young man.

One day, the Steipler arrived at Yeshivas Bais Meir in Bnei Brak in search of a student who had just announced his engagement. The Steipler had seen a notice on Harav

Dessler Street about an apartment for rent, and had hurried to inform the *chassan* of the news.

THE STEIPLER once discovered an interpretation of an especially perplexing Rambam which pleased him so much that he was happy for days. He later found a *mishna* which mildly refuted his interpretation. Although he had five different methods of solidly answering the *mishna*'s refutation, he refused to print his concept for fear that in Heaven its veracity could be challenged. Similarly the Steipler avoided the term "nonetheless," so common in contemporary novellae.

A rabbi in London found the words "This is an exceedingly great mistake" scrawled in the margin of a page in one of the Steipler's books. The rabbi was aghast at the temerity of the individual writing such a critique, until he learned that it was the Steipler himself who had written those words; in fact, many volumes with similar objections can be found in Kollel Chazan Ish in Bnei Brak.

On one occasion, the Steipler, arriving early for the *chupah* of the Brisker Rav's son, asked for directions to a nearby synagogue where he might learn during the brief interval prior to the commencement of the ceremony. The Steipler's absorption in learning, however, ran its natural course. His name was called out for a blessing at the *chupah,* but he could not be found. It wasn't until several hours later that the Steipler, deeply engrossed in study, realized that he was in Tel Aviv and had totally "over-learned" the reason for having traveled there in the first place.

As unmindful as he might have been of his own needs, the Steipler had a remarkable capacity for recollection when it came to others:

Not too long ago, the Steipler appeared at a Bar Mitzva celebration in Bnei Brak at precisely the time indicated on the invitation. It had already been several years since the Steipler had ceased venturing out of his house to attend a *simcha* outside of his immediate family. The family of the Bar Mitzvah boy, and the handful of early arrivals, were astounded to see him, and not a little frightened.

What dire circumstances could have prompted the great Rav to attend this particular *simcha?* The Steipler asked the father of the boy for a few minutes of privacy with his son, then conferred briefly with the Bar Mitzvah boy and left. The family's astonishment was in no way diminished by the Bar Mitzvah boy's explanation: Once, when he was seven years old, he had *davened* in the Lederman shul in the same *minyan* as the Steipler. The Steipler had glanced at the book in the boy's hand and had become irate: it appeared to the Steipler that the boy was learning instead of praying, a deviation which had earned the child a stern rebuke.

The Steipler later discovered, however, that the boy had indeed been praying, but that his prayer book was laid out in the form of a *gemara,* with text in the center of the page surrounded by commentaries. The Steipler had inquired after the boy, his family and his age. He had wished to ask the boy's forgiveness, but since minors "may not forgive," he had made a mental note which was still legible six years later. Thus, when the night of the boy's Bar Mitzva arrived and the child became a halakhic adult, the Steipler hastened to ask his forgiveness for the unjust reprimand of six years earlier.

On another occasion, the Steipler took a taxi to the Ponevezh Yeshiva for the purpose of paying back two *lirot* to an *avrech;* the young man had provided him with that amount a few days earlier when the Steipler was caught without change to give a beggar.

TOWARDS THE END of the Steipler's life, he endured a great deal of physical suffering, but throughout his existence he endured mental anguish no less tortuous: He was exceedingly disturbed that he once had quoted a *Birkei Yosef* during the annual *shiur* he delivered on the *yahrzeit* of the Chazon Ish, always very well attended, and had failed to mention that the *Birkei Yosef* was brought to his attention by Rabbi Akiva Eiger. "I have thus misled the public," he chastised himself, "and they may erroneously think me an expert in the words of the *Birkei Yosef.*"

The Steipler's physical afflictions, at his life's conclusion, were aggravated by the fact that they hampered his ability to learn. When the Steipler was admitted to the Tel Hashomer Hospital in Tel Aviv, the chief physician wished to connect him to a particular apparatus. The Steipler objected, however, for fear that the machine would interfere with his learning. The doctor wrote in large letters on a piece of paper: "Rabbi, this is a matter of life and death!" The Steipler responded that there was no greater question of life and death for him than whether or not he would be able to learn...

On the day of his funeral, a procession gathered, such as Bnei Brak had never before witnessed. Municipal employees had worked through the night preparing the streets for the anticipated crowds, but the crowds far exceeded their expectations. Two hundred thousand mourners poured into Bnei Brak. Hundreds of taxis, buses and cars from across the country created a traffic jam of colossal proportions.

The masses escorted the deceased all the way to the cemetery where he was laid to rest alongside his brother-in-law, the Chazon Ish. Many lingered at the gravesite to offer silent prayers. And some even wrote requests on pieces of paper — just as they had always done in the Steipler's phenomenal lifetime.

The Steipler's Advice on Chinuch

FOR THE CHILD

✺   The Steipler contended that *chinuch yeladim* commences with childbirth. He would personally visit newborn babies in order to stimulate them and gauge their reaction.

✺   The Steipler was particular that a baby boy should wear a *kippa* or some covering on his head from the moment he is born. He likewise believed a baby's hands should be washed for *netilas yadaim* in the morning, from the very first day.

✺   From an early age a child must get accustomed to the idea that he cannot have everything he desires.

✺   Parents must demonstrate their disapproval of a child's misbehavior.

✺   A child should never receive corporal punishment unless he has damaged or destroyed something.

✺   Good behavior should be complimented and rewarded. The Steipler encouraged his grandchildren's good behavior with every kind of incentive, from money, to candy, to toys, to drawings — which he drew himself — anything except dolls which he detested for they are *tsuras adam*.

This section was translated and compiled with the help of Yeshivas Kehillas Yaakov; a yeshiva where this advice is implemented.

❀ Parents should never boast of or praise the accomplishments or intelligence of their children (whether or not in the child's presence) to anyone but close family members.

❀ A child who is neglectful (e.g., leaves the tap running, does not turn off the lights) demonstrates that he has not received adequate *chinuch*.

❀ One of the most educational experiences for a child is being present in shul during the *Yomim Noraim* and *Simchas Torah*. For this reason parents should be particular about bringing their children to a well-attended shul or yeshiva at these times, even if a smaller *minyan* is graced by a great *tzaddik*.

❀ The Steipler advocated relating the stories of *tzaddikim* to children. He treated books which portrayed the lives of the righteous as holy material.

❀ Teachers must take care not to overburden their students. Accordingly, *cheder* teachers should *not* instruct in Yiddish if that is not the child's mother tongue. (It would be advisable, however, to occasionally insert certain Yiddish words and expressions into the lesson so that the child will have some familiarity with the language as this can help him in later learning endeavors.)

❀ The Steipler strongly encouraged children to study (not memorize) *mishnayos*. He was also particular that a child should be competent in arithmetic, writing and self-expression.

FOR BAR MITZVA AGE

❀ He blessed every bar mitzva boy לא לבטל את הזמן. He maintained that if the child will not waste his time he will develop into an אדם גדול.

❀ For a boy who has no desire to learn he advocated learning for just fifteen minutes, followed by a brief recess before beginning the next fifteen-minute session.

❀ A proper amount of sleep (no less than eight hours per day) is vital for one's mental health. Just as a carpenter and an electrician guard the tools of their trade, so must the yeshiva student protect his mind for it is the tool of his trade.

❀ The Steipler calculated that sleeping for eight hours plus adequate time for prayers and meals leaves twelve hours a day for learning.

❀ The fundamental basis for learning is understanding *pshat;* the primary pitfall of learning is struggling to develop novel concepts. A *chiddush* or *peirush* must never be suggested before the *pshat* is solidly understood. Under no circumstances would the Steipler tolerate מערכות, likewise he despised חבורות. He saw no value in a *shiur* unless it dealt with *pshat*.

❀ The proper way to answer a question on a *Tosafos,* for example, even on the last line of a *Tosafos* is by first clarifying the relevant gemara. Afterwards Rashi is to be explained and then — and only then — is *Tosafos* to be elucidated, starting at its beginning. In order to properly understand the answer to a question the student must be urged to overcome his reluctance or impatience to listen to an explanation he imagines he has already mastered.

❀ The Steipler was convinced that most questions emerge from a faulty understanding of *pshat.* If there is a slight misunderstanding at the beginning, he feared, there will be no comprehension at the end.

❀ Four חזרות (the customarily accepted minimum for reviewing what has been learned) should not be equated with "reviewing." "Review" only begins after the fourth time.

FOR THE YOUNG MAN

❀ The Steipler believed that yeshiva bochurim should marry young מדינא דגמרא. It was his contention that one's learning may be divided into two parts: *Limud HaYeshiva* and *Limud HaKollel.* The aim of the first is to produce a *ben Torah;* the aim of the second, to produce a *talmid chacham.* A yeshiva, he maintained, cannot create a *talmid chacham.*

❀ University must be avoided at all costs for college study entails heresy. He advised American students, pressured to attend college, to begin instead studies toward rabbinic ordination in the hope of at least deferring matriculation.

FOR THE TEACHER

☘ His instructions to a *maggid shiur* were simple: דער עיקר איז, מען דארף גוט גוט גוט מסביר זיין, כדי מען זאל גוט גוט גוט פארשטיין. "You must explain very very *very* well in order for the material to be *understood* very very very well."

☘ A *maggid shiur* must understand that there is no need to present and it is best to avoid presenting self-composed novellae. To explain an *Ohr Somayach* or a *K'tzos* is preferable to suggesting original ideas. The fundamental principle is not to overtax the students. A simple answer to a simple question is immeasurably better than an intricate response comprised of multiple strands of thought woven into a tapestry of reasoning.

☘ If a *maggid shiur* has even the slightest doubt about a particular thought he should not mention it during his shiur.

☘ Overcrowded *shiurim* are the bane of yeshivos. A *maggid shiur* cannot possibly award proper attention to, or be aware of the progress of his students if there are too many.

A Rebbe's Warmth
Reb Moshe Horowitz

A Rebbe's Warmth

LUBAVITCH of New York, Viznitz of Bnei Brak, Belz of Jerusalem. Although all these famed chassidic courts originated in White Russia, Hungary and Galicia respectively, their juxtaposition to the names of the cities in which they were reestablished in the post-war era does not seem unnatural. "The chassidic court of Boston of Brooklyn," however, strikes an odd chord. How could Boston — not a shtetl in Europe but a thriving metropolis in New England — produce a chassidic Rebbe, and what could possibly have compelled him to pull up stakes and resettle his court in Brooklyn?

The answer is a lesson in Providence. In the early 1900's, Reb Moshe HaLevi Horowitz's father, Reb Pinchas (*der Alter Bostoner Rebbe*) was advised by his uncle, the noted Llelover Rebbe, to journey to America. Reb Pinchas was appalled at the thought of leaving the Holy Land for what was reputed to be a "*treife medina*" — a land devoid of *kedushah*.

Loathe to heed his sagacious uncle's advice, he tarried in *Eretz Yisrael* until a major *din Torah* involving Jerusalem's residents was about to be adjudicated in Europe. The young scholar was dispatched abroad to represent his fellow Jerusalemites.

The trip was fraught with danger. During the return voyage, he was apprehended by hostile authorities in Salonika, Greece and incarcerated. A local Sephardi rabbi organized Reb Pinchas's escape and concealed him on a cargo ship headed for ... America!

Chassidim in Boston, Massachusetts beseeched Reb Pinchas to become their Rebbe, and the young stowaway complied. He established a *beis midrash* in Boston and there he remained until the late 1930s. The hardships of religious observance outside of the New York area compelled the "Bostoner Rebbe" to resettle in the Williamsburg section of Brooklyn. Years later his younger son, Reb Levi Yitzhak returned to New England to succeed him as "the Bostoner." Reb Moshe, his older son, became "the Bostoner Rebbe of Brooklyn" and his chassidic court continues to flourish to this very day.*

&

WHAT ARE THE LIMITS of *kiruv*? How far should one reach out to a fellow Jew to try and draw him close? Halachic responsa on this matter exist but it is difficult to set firm guidelines for human interaction. Perhaps nothing would be more instructive than a *Ma'aseh Rav,* or in this case, a *Ma'aseh Rebbe.*

A seventh-generation descendant of the Baal Shem Tov, the Bostoner Rebbe, Grand Rabbi Moshe HaLevi Horowitz, *zt"l,* demonstrated throughout a lifetime of *kiruv* the answer to this question. His example serves not only to inspire but to dispel common myths: everyone, from

* The stories herein are true and, like the other stories in this volume, are printed with the express permission of the family. Personal details have been altered so as to ensure the privacy of the individuals involved.

humble tinsmiths to righteous scholars, must do their share to bring others closer to religion and help them to lead a life richer in Torah observance. No Jew is "too busy" or "too pious" to be absolved from the mitzvah. And no Jew is "too far gone" or "too undeserving" to return to the fold.

JACK COOPER had an easy mail route: just sixteen square blocks covering one of New York's densely-populated religious neighborhoods. Most of Central Borough Park took little notice of their punctual, dependable mailman; with his clean, pressed uniform and bulging mailbag he looked about as conspicuous as a Westchester commuter in a grey flannel suit. His quiet demeanor and bland features rendered him even less remarkable to the residents he served so faithfully. One resident, however, did take note, as he did of any other Jew who crossed his threshold.

It also happened that this particular Mr. Occupant, better known as the Bostoner Rebbe of Brooklyn, received an inordinate amount of mail. There were letters from chassidim; requests for medical referrals from people who confused him with his brother, the Bostoner Rebbe of Massachusetts; an endless stream of invitations to *simcha*s; and the regular bulk of solicitations which finds its way to every prominent Torah authority.

Jack did not mind this extra burden, for the Rebbe always managed to relieve him of burdens of a different sort, the kind that are often harder to bear than the heaviest load. With a pleasant word on his lips and a sincere look in his eyes, the Rebbe always asked after Mrs. Cooper and the Coopers' boy, Shimon. His concern for Jack and his family was genuine and Jack, sensing this, would regularly unburden himself to the Rebbe and, just as regularly, receive sound advice.

Not unusual for the area he served, Jack Cooper was a religious Jew, although an unlettered one. He had never attended a yeshiva and did not even know how to learn; in fact, since graduating from public school some thirty years earlier, Jack had not read a single book of any sort. This was no particular embarrassment for him as Jack was a simple man, honest and hardworking, not intelligent enough to seek intellectual pursuits but wise enough to want a good Jewish education for his only son. He had therefore enrolled Shimon in a local yeshiva, on the advice of a neighbor whose own children attended there.

THE BOSTONER REBBE had never met his mailman's son, but he made a point of inquiring every so often about the boy's progress. On one such occasion the Rebbe was alarmed by Jack's response.

"Rabbi, I gotta tell ya, he just ain't doin' so good in school."

"That's terrible, Jack," the Rebbe commiserated. "Have you tried getting him a tutor?"

"Nah, I don't got that kinda dough. Anyway, they called us up to tell us we gotta take Shimon out."

"Did you speak with his teacher?"

"I don't know who his teacher is, I don't know who anybody is over there. All I know is they don't want him in their yeshiva so we gotta take him out."

"Where will you enroll him?"

"They told the wife that there ain't no yeshiva that will take him, so I guess we gotta send him to public school."

That was all the Rebbe had to hear. He thanked Jack for the mail and immediately telephoned the yeshiva. First he spoke to Shimon's teacher and then heard the same story from the principal.

Naturally the principal deeply valued the Rebbe's intervention, but he regretted, emphatically, that in this case nothing could be done to keep the student in the school. Shimon was an illiterate fifth grader. He spent the entire day staring out the window or playing with the cord of the venetian blind.

"We were mistaken," the principal explained, "in not expelling him years ago. He cannot read even on a first grade level, he cannot add two numbers together, I doubt if he knows in which direction to open a *chumash*. The only reason Shimon Cooper was promoted after having been left back for three years is that he was too tall for the furniture in the lower grades.

"I appreciate the Rebbe's concern, but we have standards here and this Cooper boy simply does not measure up."

The Rebbe could not be swayed from his mission. Using all of his influence and committing himself to personally undertake responsibility for the boy's remedial improve- ment — a promise he could no more than hope to fulfill — the Bostoner Rebbe launched a campaign to save the spiritual life of Shimon Cooper.

ALTHOUGH AT EVERY TURN the Rebbe encoun- tered obstacles of one sort or another, he was undeterred, and the yeshiva administration suddenly found itself in a quandary. They never imagined that the Rebbe would fight so hard, or be so insistent about a child who was neither a relative nor the son of a congregant.

Still, they claimed that they were compelled to expel Shimon, not only for the good of the school, but ultimately, for the boy's own good as well. (The Rebbe failed to see how any "good" could come out of the youngster's attending public school.) They further contended that they had the parents' tacit approval for their decision. The Coopers had never telephoned to inquire about their son, had never attended a PTA meeting, indeed had not even uttered a word of protest when they had been informed that Shimon would have to leave the yeshiva. "Isn't it obvious," the principal concluded, "that the Coopers agree that their son is wasting his time in yeshiva?"

The only thing that was obvious, the Rebbe thought to himself, was that the Coopers were too simple to grasp what was happening or what was at stake, but this he would not say to the principal. The faculty had a low enough opinion of Shimon's intelligence; they did not require further corroboration of their claim that he was ineducable.

The Coopers, for their part, felt they had given yeshiva education a fair chance. They themselves had never received a Jewish education and while it would have been "nice" for their son to attend yeshiva, even at great expense to them, they had yet to see any justification for the effort. In fact, they viewed the yeshiva's initiative as a blessing in disguise, and the Rebbe's intervention an unbidden intrusion into their private lives. All the Rebbe's dire warnings regarding Shimon's future sounded preposterous to them, since they had both attended public school as children yet had not become less religious.

Shimon, too, had no regrets about leaving yeshiva — a place where he had no friends and was woefully bored. The opportunity to attend a coed school, where classes were dismissed much earlier in the afternoon, was enticing and he began to look forward to that seemingly "carefree" life.

In short, the Bostoner Rebbe was fighting against an administration which claimed that the Rebbe was placing one student's needs above the welfare of the entire yeshiva, against parents who opposed his intervention, and against a boy who was virtually engineering his own expulsion.

THE REBBE invited the Coopers over to his house to try and impress upon them the fact that a Jewish education was critical and that it was worth any sacrifice. He explained that public school today is different from the way it was thirty-five years ago. A public school in New York, he repeatedly emphasized, was a haven for drug abusers and a place where behavior antithetical to Judaism was the norm. But his words fell on deaf ears.

The Rebbe then tried his luck with Shimon. In the same patient manner he used to address the parents, he now spoke to their son, although he knew his chances of success were slim. To his surprise, the Rebbe soon detected that Shimon was not as educationally subnormal as the yeshiva had claimed. Shimon understood very well what the Rebbe was saying, but displayed a strong aversion to scholastic activity, an aversion inconsonant with his apparent intellectual level.

The Rebbe had an idea. He took a pen and a slip of paper and wrote the word B O Y in block letters. "Shimon," he cajoled in a soft tone, "can you tell me what it says on this piece of paper?"

Shimon stared at the slip of paper and concentrated on the letters. He tried to read the simple three-letter word, but was unable. The Rebbe positioned himself closer to the boy and, indicating the first letter, asked, "Can you tell me what letter this is?"

"B," Shimon quickly replied.

The Rebbe heaved a sigh of relief. "And what letter is this?" he asked, pointing to the middle letter.

"O."

"And this?"

"Y."

The Rebbe warmly complimented Shimon, and a bashful grin appeared on a face which was clearly not accustomed to recognition.

"Shimon," the Rebbe said, placing a solicitous hand on the boy's shoulder, "do you mind if I speak with your parents alone for a few minutes? Go into the kitchen and see if the Rebbetzen is finished baking her cookies."

T HE BOSTONER REBBE told the Coopers that he now understood why their son had not succeeded in yeshiva. Shimon had a learning disability.

"What does that mean?" Jack asked anxiously.

"It means that your son is neither stupid nor unintelligent. He simply has difficulty in putting letters together to make whole words. Because of this problem, he is frustrated and feels incapable of achieving success in any academic endeavor, a feeling which has been reinforced — unintentionally, I'm sure — by his teachers. If this problem is given proper attention, it can be overcome and I would venture that Shimon will amaze us with his scholastic ability.

"There is someone who davens in our *shtiebel*," the Rebbe continued, "who works in this field. I will see to it, God willing, that he arranges lessons for Shimon. If this problem can be corrected quickly, it will not be necessary for Shimon to leave the wholesome environment of a yeshiva for a Gentile school."

The Coopers seemed relieved to have had the matter

taken out of their hands. Whatever happened with Shimon's future, they said, was now the Rebbe's problem. The yeshiva administration, however, was less easily won over.

ALTHOUGH THE BOSTONER REBBE'S confidence in Shimon's scholastic potential was not shared by the faculty of the yeshiva, he persevered in his struggle to save a soul. He fought for "another chance" at first daily, then weekly, and at last monthly until Shimon's slow but steady improvement was apparent to all concerned. And all the while, he personally oversaw Shimon's special tutoring and gave encouragement to the family.

The Rebbe was not mistaken in his analysis. Once the proper methods were adopted to alleviate the learning disability, the results were fast in coming. The Rebbe's *nachas* was second only to Shimon's own.

Shimon went on to read, to study and to learn Torah. And when he was finally awarded his hard-won high school diploma, he could not forget the troubles of his youth. On the advice of his mentor and surrogate father, the Bostoner Rebbe, he went on to teach children with learning disabilities in a number of Brooklyn yeshivos.

Drawing Close

"HEY, GRAMPA!" This was the second epithet to be hurled in the Bostoner Rebbe's direction. The first had been "Hey, Greybeard," but it was the second that made him pause in midstride. The Rebbe, it was well known, was a very modest man. He was also a venerable Torah authority and chassidic leader and unaccustomed to being addressed by that title — and certainly not in that tone.

He turned toward the source of the shouting to see two of New York's Finest frisking a hirsute youth in bleached-out jeans and a sloganed T-shirt diagonally across the street. The Rebbe crossed over to investigate.

The youth, in his late teens, lolled languidly against a brick wall, with apparent disdain for the patrolman examining the contents of his pockets.

"Come to rescue me, Grampa?" the boy challenged in a flippant tone.

"Do you need rescuing, my son?" the Rebbe countered, "and why do you call me 'Grampa'? If indeed we are related, then I would be happy to offer any assistance I can."

"Hey — I don't need no old coot to rescue me!" the teenager insisted with as much indignation as the circumstances allowed. "Beat it, old man. Go back to your synagogue!"

T HE REBBE was only slightly taken aback by the youth's brash tone. A man renowned for his equanimity, the Bostoner Rebbe could not be unsettled, even by a young hood about to be arrested. On the contrary, the Rebbe's composure seemed to unsettle this tough teenager. The Rebbe knew that Providence had "invited" him to the site, for a reason, and he was curious to know what it was.

"You still didn't tell me why you called me 'Grampa,' young man."

"I don't owe you no explanations!" the boy replied, but could not restrain himself from answering the warm, gentle Rebbe's question. "You look like a picture I seen of my Grampa — alright?" The defiant final note, unwarranted by the circumstances, came out only through force of habit, the Rebbe thought, but he was far more interested in the boy's words than his tone.

"If I remind him of his grandfather," the Rebbe mused, "this youngster is in more trouble than meets the eye." Aloud he said, "Pardon me," addressing the police officer, "but are you taking this young man into custody? Has he committed a crime?"

"Well, Rabbi," the older of the two began, "we come here on this two-eleven, see? 'Robbery In Progress.' An' this here kid, he's in a darned awful rush to flee from the scene of the crime. So we start pursuing' him an' let me tell ya, this kid can run! Me an' Frank, here, we ain't had a workout like that since we pursued that 'sneaker-boy' clear across the

Brooklyn Bridge, am I right Frank or what?" Frank nodded in agreement.

THE REBBE waited patiently for a gap in the patrolman's recitation to inquire, "Is there any evidence that he was involved in this robbery?"

"Nah," Frank replied, "he's clean. But we're taking him downtown for questioning."

Throughout this exchange, the youth maintained his apathetic stance, casually flipping a coin in the air to further demonstrate his total disinterest in the goings on. "What is your name, young man?" the Rebbe asked but the boy only stared at him vacantly. Frank seized a fistful of the boy's shirtfront and demanded, "Don't you got no respect, punk? Answer the old man!"

"What if I don't," the teenager sneered, "I'll get another dose of 'police brutality'?" Frank released his shirt abruptly. "The name's Goldberg," he said, confirming the Rebbe's suspicions, "Mark Goldberg. What's it to you?"

Turning to the patrolmen, the Rebbe said, "Officers, I am Moshe Horowitz from Forty-ninth Street. Your lieutenant and I are well acquainted. If you would be so kind as to release Mr. Goldberg to my custody, I shall take full responsibility and you gentlemen can get on with your vital work." The patrolmen shrugged their shoulders, aware that they had no hard evidence against the "punk," and handed him over to the softspoken Rabbi. Just then, the radio in their patrol car squawked to life. They climbed into the sedan and drove off without even a backward glance.

Mark thrust his hands into his pockets and said, "Good move Rabbi. See ya around." He spun on his heels and headed down the block.

"Just one moment, young man," the Rebbe said in a stern tone. "I have assumed custody of you, so you are to come with me."

Mark, not one to obey orders, immediately backed down when he saw the Rebbe's adamant expression. "Okay," he surrendered, "that's cool," and with a mock-gallant sweep of his arm, stepped aside to allow the Rebbe to pass. "Age before beauty, man — so you lead the way." The Rebbe *krechtzed* a mighty "oiy" and started for home with his charge in tow.

ALONG THE WAY, the Rebbe asked Mark if he ever had a Jewish education. The youth simply rolled his eyes. Taking that for a "no," the Rebbe said, "Well, then, I have a great deal to teach you." Goldberg paled visibly. From the expression on the boy's face, the Rebbe could tell he was wondering if he might not have been better off "downtown" with Frank.

As they approached the steps of the Bostoner's home, the Rebbe announced, "First we'll eat supper." "Now you're talking, man!" Mark said with genuine enthusiasm, certain this meant a reprieve. The Rebbe went over to a closet and returned with a large yarmulka. He extended it to Mark, who stared at it with revulsion. "That beanie's for me?"

"Of course," the Rebbe replied. "Now, our first lesson is how to wash our hands before we eat..."

"Gimme a *break,* old man! If I feel like washing my hands, I'll wash my hands and I don't need no whack-o greybeard to show me how!"

The Rebbe, pretending he had not heard, led his guest into the kitchen where he instructed him how to wash and how to make the blessing. He went to great lengths to explain that one may not interrupt between washing and eating — even to speak, and the few seconds of silence between washing and breaking bread provided a welcome respite from Mark's nonstop tirade, the thrust of which was that "this religion trip" was not for him.

It did not matter. The Bostoner Rebbe had every intention of showing Mark the sights on a "trip" the boy clearly preferred not to travel. An unappreciative Goldberg was to have greater exposure to the Rebbe than some of the Bostoner's closest chassidim.

AFTER SUPPER, the Bostoner Rebbe showed his ward — so recently detained by the police on suspicion of robbery — to a bedroom containing many valuable items. "This will be your room," he said as if welcoming an honored guest. Mark was overwhelmed, not by the Rebbe's gracious hospitality and generosity, but by his naiveté. And the test proved too great for him.

His first night at the Rebbe's residence, he began to "case the joint," prowling out of his room when he was sure that everyone in the household was asleep. He had already emptied his bedroom of valuables and stashed them in a pillowcase under the bureau. But just when his gaze fell on some silver ornaments which he thought might bring him a tidy sum, he heard a sound that made his heart pound loudly in his chest. Mark peered into the room from where the noise emanated and discovered his host reading aloud in a strange language from an oversized book. The would-be thief could not have known that the Rebbe was merely engaged in Talmudic research, but the fear of being apprehended in mid-felony sent him tiptoeing back to bed to await a better opportunity.

Over the next few days Mark learned that this "Rabbi" whom he had stopped on the street was no ordinary cleric. His host was none other than "The Bostoner Rebbe," whatever that meant.

One thing it did mean, was that an incredible number of men in chassidic garb constantly swarmed all over Mark's newly-staked turf. There was always someone and his brother-in-law who wished to visit, consult, or seek the blessing of the Rebbe. All this interference placed a definite crimp in Mark's style; still he found time to snatch almost anything that wasn't nailed down. The challenge he now faced was finding a way to abscond with the loot undetected.

AFTER FOUR DAYS in the Rebbe's court, Goldberg had more than he could handle of piety and Jewish observance, but three square meals a day and a warm bed were certainly an improvement over cold pizza and a park bench. Furthermore, he had not yet solved the problem of his getaway since the Rebbe's nocturnal Talmudic research continued unabated. One other factor made him contemplate and recontemplate his decision to leave: as difficult as it was for Mark to admit it to himself, deep down he had taken a liking to his "Rabbi."

It was evident that the Rebbe liked him too. Mark was well aware that many of the chassidim who entered the Rebbe's court did not share the Rebbe's feelings towards him. Although they always communicated in Yiddish, which he did not understand at all, certain nuances and gestures did not require translation.

As far as Mark could tell, the Rebbe was as oblivious to their protests as he was about Mark's own constant gripes regarding the dictates of religion. Mark was intrigued: was the Rebbe the absent-minded type, the saintly type, or just hopelessly naive.

A lot of things were "missing" from the house, but the Rebbe refrained from leveling any accusations. Mark felt certain that, no matter how much time the Rebbe spent studying his books, he *had* to know about the pilfering, if not through the comments of others then by empirical evidence. The Rebbe was "Cool" all right, frustratingly cool. Is this some psychological ploy, Mark wondered, or is he just giving me enough rope to hang myself? Mark vowed not to underestimate the Rebbe or be taken in by his unassuming façade.

WHEN THE REBBE received a cassette in the mail of a well-received lecture which he had delivered, all the members of the household were anxious to hear it. But the tape recorder could not be found. This time, the family felt, the situation had gone too far. They brought their grievance to the Rebbe, but all he had to say was: "There really isn't time now to listen to the tape. We can wait until later."

Mark began to get nervous. The Rebbe's absolute confidence made Mark suspect that a trap had been set for him and he'd walked right into it. He surreptitiously replaced the tape recorder and several of his more valuable items of "loot."

The Rebbe, for his part, had no such trap set. He simply intended to wait for Mark to turn around. He held long discussions with him and continued to cater to his needs — physical and spiritual — and to try and kindle the dormant spark within Mordechai Golberg's soul. And that spark, like the sparks of so many other Jews, was eventually ignited by the warmth and affection and infinite patience of the Bostoner Rebbe.

Drawing the Far

"**I**ZZY, what's the story? Are you coming to my house for Shabbos or not? I promised my mother I'd let her know for sure by Thursday, the latest. So, what do you say?"

Sam must have asked his friend this question a dozen times. The two attended classes together at one of Manhattan's largest yeshivas, and Sam was eager for his family to meet his closest out-of-town buddy.

"Don't think I don't want to come," Izzy explained over the din of the cafeteria, "but I have three aunts in New York and two roommates who live here, not to mention a few 'prior engagements'."

The other boys at the table snickered. "Get a load of him — Mr. Popularity!" But Sam was undeterred. "Then how about next Shabbos?"

"Can't," Izzy mumbled around a mouthful of tuna fish sandwich, "I don't think I'm free until five weeks from now."

"All right, you're on in five weeks — and you can tell anyone who asks that you're taken for that Shabbos."

Avraham, eating a solitary lunch at the adjacent table, overheard the entire conversation. It was enough to destroy his already shattered ego. Avraham didn't have any Shabbos invitations, not for this week, not for next week, not for last week. In fact, the few rare weekends he'd spent at a classmate's home had been the result of his own initiative, and inviting himself was something he despised doing. If not for the fact that the alternative of spending Shabbos alone in the dormitory was so thoroughly undesirable, he might never have mustered the nerve.

AVRAHAM tried to summon his courage. He feared that whatever backbone he once had had been whittled away by these weekly humiliations. Inviting oneself, he concluded, was a no-win situation. You felt shame in the request and risked embarrassment in the response. No one was more anxious to get married than Avraham, for one simple reason: so that he would at last have a home.

He toyed with the silverware on his tray, hoping the rattling would make the others aware of his presence, but it was an exercise in futility. Everyone at school seemed to have no difficulty finding a group of friends with whom to sit in the cafeteria, and their conversations were always animated and amusing. But after more than a year in the yeshiva, Avraham remained an outsider, a loner-by-default.

Desperate, and steeling himself for the anticipated rebuff, he tried the direct approach: "Eh, excuse me. I just happened to catch the tail end of your conversation, and I was wondering if, er, maybe I could come along for Shabbos?"

Sam and his classmates exchanged an embarrassed look. "I-I guess," he stuttered after a brief lapse, "you missed the beginning of the conversation. You see, uh, basically, we're full this Shabbos, but, um, Izzy really owes us a visit, and we would have squeezed him in somehow." Sam beamed with pride at his rapid recovery, even though he'd been caught off guard. "Maybe some other time?"

Avraham looked at his classmate's face and saw no real malice there. Prejudice — yes, and something else. Fear? He decided to try again. It was perseverance that had brought him this far on the long, lonely road he'd travelled and he was not about to give up yet. "How about the Shabbos when Izzy comes in five weeks?"

Glances once again shot across the table. "We'll see," Sam replied, oh-so-casually, "Stay in touch." He then resumed his conversation as if Avraham and the moral conflict he represented had evaporated.

AVRAHAM CARLSON, a native of Saskatchewan, Canada, had been through this many times before. He was beginning to develop a tough outer shell, but inside he was bleeding. The Torah, he knew, repeatedly urged for providing extra attention and protection to a convert, but Avraham felt as if he were surrounded by Torah-illiterates, even here in this Torah academy.

Avraham tried not to allow incidents such as these to upset him. Before his conversion he had endured far greater abuse. He had come such a long way, and he wished to travel even further, but he was starved for spirituality. In addition to his personal study, he pursued any avenue which he thought might lead him to new religious heights. It occurred to him that it was this thirst that separated him from his classmates and others who were "born Jewish." Perhaps, he wondered, a Jew carries a spiritual spark in his soul while I carry only a deep void.

HIS NEED to fill that void was great, and it was that need that brought him to Brooklyn on *Lag B'Omer* eve. No one had included Avraham in their plans for the day and he'd disconsolately boarded a subway train heading for nowhere in particular. On the train, he'd overheard two chassidim discussing the Bostoner Rebbe's special *Lag B'Omer* celebrations; the temptation to follow them had been irresistible.

Lag B'Omer in "Boston" is truly special. It is the only place in the New York area, maybe in all of America, where a *hadlakah* is made. The joy and songs so much associated with the festivities in Jerusalem and Miron, pervade this bastion of chassidic tradition. Scores of chassidim dance around the modest bonfire to the tune of "*Bar Yochai*" until the wee hours of the morning.

The impressario of the festivities is naturally the Bostoner Rebbe, who also presides as well over the "*chalakos*" — the first haircuts of three-year-old boys — performed the following morning.

Like his father who conducted the first "*Rebbeshe Tisch*" in Brooklyn forty years earlier, Reb Moshe HaLevi Horowitz was keenly attuned to his chassidim and sensitive to every nuance and gesture. He could easily tell who sang with a full heart, and who participated without enthusiasm, distracted by personal problems.

Like a magnet to a lodestone, the Rebbe was drawn to Avraham among the myriad spectators and participants. That look of dejection he wore could never have escaped the sharp eyes of the saintly man whose life was dedicated to spreading joy and solace to his People.

THE REBBE broke from the circle of his followers to welcome the young man who looked so forlorn.

Wordlessly, he gripped Avraham's hands and drew him towards the center of the crowd. The Rebbe's warmth enveloped him. Avraham felt his spirit soar. The void in his heart filled to bursting with the love which the Rebbe radiated and the two danced and rejoiced all night long, celebrating *Lag B'Omer* in this most meaningful way.

The Rebbe insisted that Avraham be his guest for Shabbos, an invitation which Avraham most gratefully accepted. It turned out to be the second most momentous decision of his life: that invitation led to another, and another, and from a regular Shabbos guest, he became a genuine *ben bayis* and confidant of the Rebbe.

But the Rebbe was not content with having rescued a lost soul. He wanted more for this very special youth. He was not satisfied until he had arranged the one thing that Avraham needed more than anything else — a wife and home of his own. When at last this mission was accomplished, the Rebbe's — and Avraham's — joy knew no bounds.

The Lion's Share
Reb Leib Gurwicz

Reb Leib Gurwicz:
The Lion's Share

Leadership is one ship which cannot pull into a safe port in a storm. Rabbi Leib ("lion" in Yiddish) Gurwicz assumed the lion's share in leading British Jewry, as dean of its foremost yeshiva. The roar that issued forth from the Gateshead *Rosh Yeshiva* heralded, in the words of the Chofetz Chaim, redemption for the Torah community of England and salvation for the local level of learning. In actuality, the confluence of circumstances which led to his immigration to England represented a "redemption and salvation" for himself as well.

❦Rue Britannia

Like many *roshei yeshiva*, Eliyahu Lopian bore the financial as well as the spiritual yoke of his yeshiva. Responsibility for the material support of the institution resulted in frequent trans-European trips. On one such fundraising mission, Reb Elya had traversed a great deal of Europe and was in Germany on the last leg of his journey. Just before departing, he asked a local Jew for directions. The latter responded, "*Rebbe*, come with me and I will show you the way." When they came to a dark alley, a gun was placed at Reb Elya's head and the proverbial option offered.

His money gone, Reb Elya was now in a bind. He could not return to the same villages he had solicited just one month earlier, but he also could not return home empty-handed. The one and only alternative lay across the sea in England.

England at that time, from the perspective of an observant Jew, was a world apart. It's only connection to Europe was its geographic proximity. As far as a Lithuanian *rosh yeshiva* was concerned, it might just as well have been thousands of miles away. British Jewry was by and large irreligious and thoroughly ignorant of Torah learning and *mitzvos*.

REB ELYA decided to employ the *Goral HaGra** to determine if he should embark on the trip. The *goral* landed on the verse: "I will go down with you to Egypt and I will surely bring you up again..." (*Bereishis* 46:4), an apparently clear indication that he should proceed with the journey.

When Reb Elya arrived in England he encountered a friend of his from Kelm, Rabbi Aharon Bakst — the *Rosh Yeshiva* and founder of the Etz Chaim Yeshiva in London. "Reb Elya," began Rabbi Bakst, "I must travel to Europe for a short visit. Perhaps you would be so kind as to fill in for me in my absence?"

Rabbi Bakst never returned to England. Reb Elya was left with a yeshiva to direct, another yeshiva to fund and a wife and thirteen children back in Kelm. What was he to do? He realized that the yeshiva in Kelm could survive without him, for he was not its sole *rosh yeshiva*. Furthermore,

---

* The *Goral HaGra*, literally, "lottery of the Vilna Gaon," is a method of determining action in accord with the implications of a biblical verse.

there was no dearth of *roshei yeshiva* in interbellum Lithuania.

And so in 5688 (1928) Reb Elya sent for his family to pack their belongings and join him in England. After arriving at a difficult decision, its execution became even harder...

Reb Elya's father-in-law, Rabbi Yitzhak Dovid Rotman, a renowned *tzadik* who lived in Jerusalem, heard from an Englishman what the norms of religious observance in England were at that time.

"I thought I took a God-fearing son-in-law!" he wrote in fury to Reb Elya. "How could you abandon Lithuania for such a wilderness?!" To his daughter he wrote even stronger words: "If your husband does not agree to return from London to Kelm you must insist on a divorce!"

But she didn't heed her father's counsel. The Lopians managed to raise their thirteen children with the highest Torah standards despite their presence on British soil. Local *shiduch* opportunities, however, presented a problem.

I N 5694 (1934) Reb Elya and his eldest daughter, Leiba, returned to Europe in search of a suitable match. Already long-removed from the Lithuanian scene, Reb Elya turned for suggestions to his close friend from his days in the Kelmer *Beis HaMussar,* Reb Yeruchom Levovitz, the *Mashgiach* of the Mirrer Yeshiva.

There were many older unmarried students at the Mirrer Yeshiva because of the shortage of appropriate matches;* however, Reb Yeruchom rejected them all but one particular young man who had already left the Yeshiva. He had been one of the *Mashgiach*'s favorites and his qualifications met Reb Elya's criteria: the man who would

* The Bais Yaakov girls' school system was still in its infancy.

marry Leiba had to not only excel in learning but possess innately — rather than acquired — superior character traits.

"Go to the Brisker Rav," Reb Yeruchom advised, "and ask for 'Leibeleh Malater.' He is the *illui* you are looking for. You will find in this young man more humility, acuity in learning, and fear of Heaven than in any other."

Reb Yeruchom was correct. Reb Aryeh Ze'ev (Leib) Gurwicz was just that.

The Young Lion

AT THE AGE of thirteen, Leib bade a final farewell to his family in Malat, Poland before starting off for *yeshiva ketana* in Lithuania. His father, Reb Moshe Aharon Kushelevsky, descendant of a long line of *melamdim*, was the Rabbi of this small town where few of the residents were observant. His mother was a direct descendant of the Vilna Gaon, a fact which accounted for Leib's adoption of the customs and stringencies of the *Gaon*.

Leib's willingness to leave home at bar mitzva age was typical of the self-sacrificing attitude towards learning that remained with him the rest of his life. It was no small matter for a boy so young to abandon his family knowing that he would probably never see them again. His family's impoverished circumstances and the existing means of transportation precluded any possibility of returning.*

---

* Twelve years later Leib met his brother on Tisha B'Av in Ligmiyan. This town was in Poland but its Jewish cemetery was in Lithuanian territory. Somehow the Jews managed to convince the authorities of those two contentious countries that they must visit the graveyard on Tisha B'Av. And so for hundreds of Jews separated by a tense border, the Ninth of Av became an annual holiday for family reunions and the exchange of messages.

On a cold winter morning, Leib boarded the horse and cart which would take him to the Lithuanian frontier. Once there, he would have to slip across undetected and hope that the border police weren't shooting on that day. Before saying goodbye, his father took off his only coat and handed it to his son. "How can I take your coat when I know that you will suffer in the cold?" Leib protested. "I have already learned in yeshiva," responded his father, "and am no longer on the threshold of an advancement in Torah growth as you are. Therefore, you are the one who deserves a coat..."

Leib was so inspired by his father's gesture and parting words that from the day he arrived at the famed Vilkomirer Yeshiva in Lithuania he was always the first one into the *beis midrash* and the last one to leave...

THE TIME spent in the Vilkomirer Yeshiva, headed by Reb Elyah Kramerman and Reb Leib Rubin, was pivotal in Leibeleh Malater's development. He quickly established himself as the yeshiva's most diligent student and one of its sharpest minds.

After a year and a half in Vilkomirer, Leib journeyed to Vilna in the hope of visiting his family, which had resettled there. (As part of the Treaty of Versailles, Vilna had once again become Lithuanian.) Coincidental with Leib's visit was the arrival of the Mirrer Yeshiva which, along with several other yeshivos such as Slabodka and Radin, had fled deep into Russia during World War I. Vilna was only a temporary stopover for the Yeshiva which was waiting for the situation to stabilize so that it could return to Mir.

Leib never got to see his father, who had been called back to Malat, a town which subsequently reverted to

Polish control. He did, however, become one of the youngest students to join the Mirrer Yeshiva as a result of his visit.

AFTER A FEW YEARS in the Mir, Leib had to have his Polish passport altered. Lithuania (where he was learning) had a hostile relationship with its Polish neighbor, and Polish nationals were liable for expulsion.*

The nearest passport office was in Baranovitch, where Reb Elchonon Wasserman's yeshiva was located. There was a student in the Baranovitch Yeshiva who had the necessary connections to forge a passport; however, the procedure required that Leib adopt a new name. He chose his mother's maiden name — Gurwicz — as his surname and thus was he known for the rest of his life.

While in Baranovitch, Leib decided to visit Reb Elchonon's yeshiva and entered in the middle of the *Rosh Yeshiva*'s *shiur*. During the course of the *shiur* Leib posed a question which so impressed the famous *Rosh Yeshiva* that he pleaded with Leib to remain and learn with him.

Leib obliged, but in actuality, he had no choice. Unable to pay the fee the *bochur* demanded for arranging his new passport, he committed himself to learning קצות החושן with the *bochur* for a year, in lieu of payment.

After Leib had learned in the "Mir" for eight years, the

* Actually, Leib would have preferred to travel to *Eretz Yisrael* to learn but he had sought the blessing of Rabbi Yisrael Yaakov Lubchanski for the venture. The Rabbi's words could only have been construed as a blessing if Leib were to remain where he was... With *Eretz Yisrael* no longer an option, he had to quickly rectify his status as an illegal alien.

Rosh Yeshiva, Reb Eliezer Yehuda Finkel and the *Mashgiach,* Reb Yeruchom Levovitz, to whom Leib had become very attached, recommended that he travel to study under the Brisker Rav. Once again Leib was one of the youngest among a group of towering scholars such as Rabbis Leib Mallin, Mordechai Ginsburg and Michel Feinstein. The Brisker Rav took an exceptional liking to Leib and even awarded him his greatest accolade: ר׳ לייב קען לערנען — "Reb Leib knows how to learn." Yeshiva students are well aware of how great a learning ability is implied by the Brisker Rav's compliment of "knowing how to learn..."

§The Match is Made

I T WAS AFTER Leib had been studying under the Brisker Rav for two years that Reb Eliyahu Lopian arrived in search of the *bochur* Reb Yeruchom had so highly recommended for Reb Elya's daughter. Reb Elya's visit resulted in Leib's enjoying the unusual privilege of having not only the Mirrer Yeshiva come to him, but his bride as well.

After meeting and observing the prospective groom, Reb Elya was convinced that everything that he had heard was true, and the *"shiduch"* was consummated. It was understood that the couple would wed and remain in Poland.

During the course of the engagement, however Leibs prospective mother-in-law died at the age of 49. Leiba wrote from England to her *chossan* that her mother's untimely death ruled out travelling to Poland. Even after their marriage she would be obliged to remain in England to take care of her younger siblings. The message was clear.

REB YERUCHOM, the *shadchan*, was unable to decide whether to allow Reb Leib to journey to England. He advised him to seek the aging Chofetz Chaim's counsel and blessing, and Leib complied.

Instead of a direct response, however, the Chofetz Chaim repeated the following verses three times:

> *"Blessed be He who spoke, and the world came into being; blessed be He who created the universe. Blessed be He who says and performs. Blessed be He who decrees and fulfills. Blessed be He who has mercy on the world. Blessed be He who has mercy on all creatures. Blessed be He who grants a fair reward to those who revere Him. Blessed be He who lives forever and exists eternally. Blessed be He who redeems and saves..."*

Those who were present thought that the Chofetz Chaim was repeating himself out of forgetfulness. But Leib understood that going to England would be in the category of *"Blessed be he who redeems and saves."*

AFTER A DATE was set for Leib's wedding, his *kalla* wrote with astonishment: "How can we get married in your father's absence? I insist that your father join us for the *simcha* and I suggest that all the presents and money we receive for our wedding go to paying his fare."

Leiba prevailed and a ticket was sent to Reb Moshe Aharon Kushelevsky. From the time that he arrived in England until the day he left he seemed always to be crying. The last time he had seen his son was when Leib was a thirteen-year-old boy and now he was a distinguished *talmid chacham*, getting married in England! Indeed, the only extant picture of Leib's wedding depicts the *chossan* and *kalla* and a hand tightly clutching a well-used handkerchief. The hand belonged to Reb Moshe Aharon — a man overcome with emotion.

A few years after Reb Kushelevsky returned to Europe, he met a violent death at the hands of the Nazis. The turn of events which had brought Reb Elya, and subsequently Leib to England, spared them from the entire Nazi horror.

FROM THE DAY of his marriage Leib lived in his father-in-law's home, which housed twelve children. The children loved their new brother-in-law — especially his easygoing nature. They found it difficult to relate to their father, who was totally absorbed in spiritual pursuits, and enjoyed their new surrogate parent who served the triple role of father, brother-in-law and friend all in one. Leib and Leiba's presence in the house was as necessary for the family as for themselves — their financial situation ruled out any other alternative.

Reb Leib Gurwicz delivered a *shiur* in his father-in-law's Etz Chaim Yeshiva, and also served as Rabbi of the Great Garden Synagogue in the East End of London. In that era, *chillul Shabbos* was the norm for London's Jews. For this reason Reb Leib didn't allow his children out of the house on Shabbos lest they witness the desecration which transpired in a Jewish neighborhood.

Reb Leib once related that when he came to England he noticed that the paper in which fish was wrapped was covered with handwritten Torah novellae. The proprietor of the fish store used his father's chidushim as a means of packaging the fish, as he knew of no other function for the paper...

✿ The Tin-Hut Yeshiva

A S WORLD WAR II escalated, a considerable influx of Jewish refugees began to pour onto the English coast. At that time there were two routes from Europe to England: either by a trans-Europe train and then by boat across the English channel, or by plying the North Sea and docking in northern England.

The second route existed long before the mass exodus precipitated by World War II. Sea traffic from the north resulted in the establishment of a northern port on the River Tyne, which flows from the North Sea. This port, straddling the twin cities of Newcastle and Gateshead, is separated by the river. At the turn of the century, it burgeoned into a major inland port to accommodate the increase in sea traffic.

Many Jews fleeing Europe followed this sea lane and settled in the larger of the two cities, Newcastle, where opportunities and amenities for Jews were scarce.

A small group of these Jewish settlers realized that the only way to continue in the path of their fathers and avoid the temptation of assimilation, was to break away from the Newcastle community. Accordingly, in the early 1920s, a cluster of religious Jews crossed the river and settled in Gateshead. They quickly erected a tin hut to serve as their shul not far from the river which had brought them to the British Isles.

With the semblance of a community already established around that rickety structure, they sought a *shochet* who would meet their scrupulous standards. A letter was dispatched to the Chofetz Chaim asking him to recommend a candidate. The nominee was Reb Dovid Dryan, a man who could have been employed as a *tzadik* if not for the fact that he earned his living from preparing meat.

REB DOVID viewed his slaughtering as a side line; he was chiefly engaged in fulfilling a mission. "A Jewish community must have a yeshiva," he maintained — an idea which sounded preposterous to the local residents. "Where will you get students and funding?" they questioned scornfully. But Reb Dovid was undaunted. Oblivious to their ridicule, he set out to recruit students.

> *After he succeeded in persuading one boy and his parents to join his enterprise, he felt he could begin. The yeshiva was housed in the community's tin hut shul, which was more than adequate for the initial student body. On the opening day of the "yeshiva" Reb Dovid entered Gateshead's solitary store which carried kosher items, and said, "Please put this bread and butter on the 'yeshiva's account...' "*

This first recruit served as a nucleus for the earliest students of "Yeshivas Bais Yosef," Gateshead. A yeshiva must have a *rosh yeshiva* and so Reb Dovid turned to the Chofetz Chaim to select the appropriate scholar. Rabbi Nachman Landynsky, a graduate of the Novardoker Yeshiva was the sage's choice. Only one schooled in the "outreach doctrine" of Novardok would be willing to subject himself to such an exile.

Under the leadership of Rabbi Landynsky, the Yeshiva began to grow until its enrollment numbered thirty students. In the late 1930s, however, a trickle of European emigrants began to escape to northern England, among them several *bochurim* who wished to continue their studies. Consequently, the Yeshiva began to expand and Rabbi Landynsky felt that it now needed a *mashgiach*. He offered the job to his co-Novardoker, Reb Eleazer Kahan — who accepted.

THE MATERIAL responsibilities of the Yeshiva remained in the hands of Reb Dovid Dryan. He found that the tangible existence of the Yeshiva didn't make fundraising any easier. Wherever he went, people refused to accept the new reality and greeted him with ridicule. But the Yeshiva's poverty was no laughing matter.

Another factor which impeded the Yeshiva's development was the local climate and population. The weather in Gateshead is almost perpetually cold and rainy and the air is laden with soot from extensive coal mining in the region. The clouds, like the *shtenders* of the Yeshiva, are carbon-coated and the odor of coal dust permeates the town.

The residents of the town were uneducated, ignorant coal miners who lived in drab, dismal surroundings. The town's major asset, from the perspective of the Yeshiva, was that its total absence of distractions made it conducive to learning.

With the conclusion of World War II, Gateshead — originally a haven for a select few — became a refuge for hundreds of devout Jews. The Yeshiva grew to a student body of 120 in a matter of weeks. But Reb Dovid still wasn't satisfied. A yeshiva of this size, he contended, must have a *kollel*. And a *kollel* must have a *rosh kollel*.

Rabbi Eliahu Dessler, a scholar whose profundity of thought and oratorical abilities had made a tremendous impact in London, was selected for the job. Several young men, including two of Reb Leib's brothers-in-law, Chaim Shmuel and Laib Lopian, moved from London to Gateshead to join the new *kollel*.

As the Yeshiva expanded, its staff increased. Reb Laib Lopian was chosen from the *kollel* to deliver a *shiur* and more *rebbeim* were still sought.

&Marginal Notes

I N 5709 (1948), Reb Laib Lopian wrote his brother-in-law, Rabbi Gurwicz, to join the Gateshead faculty. His acceptance not only changed his life but had a profound effect on post-war European Jewry. The students of the Gateshead Yeshiva were on a much higher level of learning than the ones he had taught for two decades in London. Only local boys attended the Etz Chaim Yeshiva in London, whereas European immigrants — who had studied in the famous *yeshivos* of Lithuania — came to Gateshead.

Shortly after Reb Leib arrived in Gateshead, Rabbi Landynsky left for America to seek medical assistance for a child. Reb Leib was never officially appointed *Rosh Yeshiva* in the absence of his predecessor, but it was clear that he was the most eminently suitable for the job.

Reb Leib once explained the expression כרחם אב על בנים — "as a father has compassion for his children" — in a way which demonstrated his conception of the role of a *rosh yeshiva*:

> "A father's compassion for his children differs from a mother's. The emotions and reactions of a mother are triggered by what she sees and experiences in the present. A father, on the other hand, looks more into the future, which results in more calculated responses. We therefore implore the Almighty to have compassion for us as a father has for his children – compassion which takes the future into account..."

Reb Leib viewed his students as sons and cared about them not only during their years in the Yeshiva, but long after. Their welfare was uppermost in his mind.

Reb Leib taught both in the classroom and by example. His phenomenal diligence was his primary lesson.

In his later years, he lived in a house across from the Yeshiva, where he made a point of learning in a room in which the windows faced the Yeshiva building. "I want my students to know how I spend my time," he explained. In that room the Rosh Yeshiva could be seen deeply engrossed in learning until late at night.

In fact, Reb Leib became so attached to that room that he refused to leave it even for a daily fifteen-minute walk. "Surely," his students argued, "the Rosh Yeshiva will be able to contemplate Torah thoughts as he walks — but eighteen hours of sitting every day must be unhealthy." But Reb Leib was afraid of getting stranded without a sefer in the midst of a walk — an eventuality which overrode the appeal of a stroll.

HIS YESHIVA SCHEDULE* included delivering a *"blatt shiur"* every day and two *"inyanim shiurim"* weekly to the advanced students. These *shiurim* were later transcribed and became monumental works.

Reb Leib was very meticulous about writing down his own thoughts as well as scholarly discourses which he had heard. When he was a student in "Mir" he asked visiting *talmidim* to relate *shiurim* their respective *roshei yeshiva* had delivered. In this way he assembled notebooks of lectures from that generation's leading Torah luminaries.

Opposed to the idea of young people printing *sefarim*, Reb Leib reasoned that since he was an elderly *rosh yeshiva*, he could allow himself the privilege, and published

---

* Reb Leib's dedication to the Yeshiva and to Torah study did not keep him from becoming the chairman of Agudath Israel's world organization. Even though this job entailed dozens of meetings and travelling across Europe, he never missed an appointment.

his first book in 1971. He entitled the *sefer* ראשי שערים —
Rashei Shearim, a title adapted from the name of the city
which hosted the Yeshiva: *shearim* means "gates" and *rosh*
means "head." (The "Baal HaMaor," who honored the city
which hosted *him*, provided Reb Leib with the idea.)

The *Rashei Shearim* are a collection of the *inyanim
shiurim* which he delivered at the Yeshiva. Reb Leib wrote
in his preface that he was publishing the books to serve as a
review for his *talmidim* — humble words from a man whose
works are viewed as masterpieces throughout the yeshiva
world.

In 1979, Reb Leib decided to print his *blatt shiurim*.
These lectures were recorded in the margins of his Gemara,
and for each study cycle** he used a brand new one.
Nevertheless, every page in every Gemara was crowded
with annotations.

Reb Leib's remarkable power of *chidush* — novel
thought — is demonstrated by the hundreds of original
thoughts proposed every time he relearned the same
Gemara he had studied dozens of times in the past. This
collection of *shiurim* was entitled ארזא דבי רב which means
"pillar of the *beis midrash*," based on his name, אריה זאב.

F OR *SUKKOS* 5737 (1977), Rabbi and Rebbitzen
Gurwicz travelled to Israel to visit their children. This
was to be his last excursion in the company of his wife. On
their return trip to Gateshead the Rebbitzen suffered a
heart attack and died in Heathrow Airport. Since the
tragedy occurred on the way back from Israel, Reb Leib
understood that Providence was telling him that she should
be buried in the Holy Land.

** A five-year study cycle of nine Gemaras is standard for most yeshivos.

Rebbitzen Leiba was buried next to her father, Reb Elya Lopian, on the Mount of Olives in Jerusalem. She was honored with a large funeral and was eulogized by Reb Leib. Before he returned to England, one of his students overheard Reb Leib mutter to himself, "I must see to it that the Yeshiva lowers my salary now that I am all alone."

Two years later, Reb Leib's children recommended to their father that he marry the widow, Rebbitzen Malka Isbee. Rebbitzen Isbee had misgivings about pursuing the *shiduch*, which would entail leaving her family in Israel and relocating to dreary Gateshead. But when she learned that Reb Leib had moved on his wedding night into a home of twelve children, she realized the kind of man he must be, and that more than compensated for all the apparent drawbacks. She referred to her husband affectionately as "my *Rosh Yeshiva*."

&# "God, He is the Lord"

F OUR YEARS after their marriage, Reb Leib suffered a stroke. His two sons at his bedside in the Newcastle Hospital were quickly joined by their brother and sister from *Eretz Yisrael*. That afternoon the *Rosh Yeshiva* lost consciousness. The doctor in charge related that since his heart was strong, it was probable that he would remain in that condition for a long time. This news sent dozens of yeshiva students — who had arrived at the hospital — back home.

Later that Wednesday afternoon the *Mashgiach* of the Yeshiva, Rabbi Mattisyahu Salomon, joined the family and suggested that they say the verses that are recited at a deathbed. The family objected, quoting the doctor that "he will remain in that condition indefinitely." Rabbi Salomon protested that it was advisable all the same.

The sons and the *Mashgiach* and the few students who remained formed exactly a *minyan*. Together they chanted the appropriate verses — the same ones that are said at the conclusion of Yom Kippur.* With tears and sobs they began to say *Shema Yisrael*. Only a nurse was left in the room scanning the screen that monitored Reb Leib's heart.

Hashem Hu HaElokim — "God, He is the Lord." With broken hearts and unmatched fervor they repeated these words seven times, their cracked voices drowning in tears. As they recited the last verse for the seventh time, the nurse gasped and dashed out of the room.

Doctors rushed in and asked everyone to leave. Ten minutes later they emerged with word that the Rabbi had passed away. On the seventh *Hashem Hu HaElokim*, the heart monitor had stopped registering — a reflection of Reb Leib's extraordinary life.

ALL HIS life he had lived by the verse: "God, He is the Lord." The Almighty brought him to Vilkomirer, sent him across Lithuania, and led him to England.

The children decided that since their mother was buried in Jerusalem, it was appropriate for their father to be buried there as well. But the only flights to Israel were for early Thursday morning or the following Sunday. Taking the Thursday flight meant that the funeral in Gateshead would have to be very rushed and they would have to leave immediately afterwards in order to reach Heathrow Airport in time.

---

* *Shema Yisrael* is recited once; *Baruch Shem K'vod* is repeated three times; and *Hashem Hu HaElokim*, seven times.

The Gateshead Rav, however, ruled that it was wholly inappropriate to make a hasty funeral for a man who devoted his entire life for Torah. The Jerusalem burial society objected vehemently, but the Rav remained firm in his ruling that the funeral could only take place in Jerusalem on Sunday night.*

The family heeded his ruling and the first part of the funeral was scheduled for Thursday afternoon in Gateshead. In the middle of the night, Zalman Margolius, a wealthy English businessman and former student of the Gateshead Yeshiva, telephoned. "I have a Gentile friend," Margolius said, "who has several private aircraft and I told him of your dilemma. He has agreed to lend us a plane so that your father may be buried in *Eretz Yisrael* before Shabbos."

THURSDAY AFTERNOON, a massive funeral was conducted in the Gateshead Yeshiva as scheduled, and later the procession headed for Newcastle Airport, where a private Gulf Stream plane was waiting. The non-Jews of the twin cities were astounded and impressed by the size and decorum of the funeral procession.

The plane took off for Stansted Airport, Essex (London) where the *aron* was taken to a heavily attended *levaya* at the Stamford Hill *Beis Hamidrash*. The crowd was so large that many could not gain entry and stood outside in the pouring rain for over two hours. The plane then departed for *Eretz Yisrael* for the final stage of the funeral. This guaranteed that the much-desired preference for burial prior to Shabbos would be achieved.

* Such a lengthy delay is unheard of in Jerusalem where the deceased are buried within hours of their death.

The residents of Jerusalem were similarly responsive to the great loss. Over 15,000 people (an unusually large number for *erev Shabbos*) crowded into the Mattersdorf neighborhood of Jerusalem. The eulogies could only emphasize that which had already been said: Reb Leib stood at the helm of European Jewry by virtue of his greatness in Torah, his selfless devotion to others, his forthrightness and humility.

The honor and manner in which the funeral was conducted attested to the worth of the man. His whole life he shunned honor and therefore merited the ultimate honor. Not only was he guided by "God, He is the Lord" all his days, but he also witnessed a rich fulfillment of the Chofetz Chaim's blessing: his travelling to England was a redemption and salvation for English Jewry, as well as a fortuity which saved his own life. Even more than that, what the Gateshead *Rosh Yeshiva* accomplished in England was in the category of "Blessed be He who has compassion for the creations."

Little wonder he merited "a fair reward to those who fear Him..."

In the Reign of Emmes
Reb Yosef Dov Soloveitchik

Reb Berel and
the Reign of Emmes

EB YOSEF DOV (Berel) Soloveitchik, the renowned dean of the Brisker Yeshiva in Jerusalem, was the scion of one of the most famous rabbinic families in Eastern Europe. What he accomplished in his brief life time was nothing less than a revolution in the contemporary concept of yeshiva study. To appreciate his contribution, however, one must first appreciate his past.

In a town called Brisk, where talmudic erudition reigned supreme and intensive learning was the ultimate value, one man rose above all others. His name was Chaim, son of Yosef Dov Halevi, Soloveitchik, better known as "Reb Chaim Brisker." Born in 5613 (1853) he became the outstanding Torah figure of his time, and generated a departure in yeshiva curriculum and methodology.

Reb Chaim's famous learning technique which has become the bedrock of higher yeshiva erudition, was his ability to itemize: שני דינים — two principles, two rules, two categories — the object and the person, the active and the passive, the general and the specific, etc. Is the "fulfillment of the commandment to destroy *chometz*" before Passover a law regarding a *Jew* who must remove *chometz* from his possession, or that the *object* of *chometz* must be destroyed during this period? By breaking everything down into specific categories, most questions and problems became either irrelevant or inapplicable.

Reb Chaim, like all of his descendants, was a true zealot — zealous about causes and zealous about his love for his fellow Jew.

> *"I am alone with nothing to eat," whimpered a woman in an advanced stage of pregnancy at the threshold of the Soloveitchik home. Reb Chaim asked his wife why the women of the town were not helping — but the Rebbitzen did not respond and pretended not to have heard the question.*

> *Reb Chaim continued to probe until the Rebbitzen disclosed that this woman's husband had abandoned her over eleven months ago... "How much more so," interjected Reb Chaim, "is she all alone and dependent upon our help. Hurry and prepare a room for her where she will be our guest for the next few weeks, and then we will provide a monthly stipend for her and the child for the coming two years..."*

> *Two weeks later a bris was held in the very same house which had lodged the mother — the guest of Reb Chaim Brisker...*[1]

* This story highlights Reb Chaim's magnanimity towards his fellow man; it does not, of course, imply that Reb Chaim condoned the woman's behavior.

YITZHAK ZE'EV — Velvel, was Reb Chaim's youngest son. In 5652 (1892) when Velvel was four years old, the Volozhiner Yeshiva (where his father, grandfather and great-grandfather had been *Roshei Yeshiva*) closed down and his family moved to Brisk. It is reasonable to assume that Velvel received a staunch resistance to the "Enlightenment movement" — which precipitated the Volozhiner Yeshiva's closing. From Brisk he inherited opposition to secular values in general, and he took the initiative to counteract them.

Steeped in Torah learning and zealous in his observance of mitzvos, Reb Velvel (the Brisker Rav) was a beacon of confidence. He didn't flinch at any intimidation from the outside world nor succumb to pressures from within.

> *Many students, along with several notables, appealed to the Brisker Rav to permit electioneering prior to the* Motzai Shabbos Kehilla *(an organization responsible to the government) ballot. "If the Rav won't allow us to broadcast our platform, the irreligious camp will win by a landslide," they argued, and the Brisker Rav grudgingly agreed.*

> *Ironically, the irreligious and the religious hired the same printer to run off their placards and literature. Apparently, for an additional fee, the printer showed the irreligious campaign organizers the text of the adherents of the Brisker Rav. The irreligious then printed an even more profanatory placard, strongly condemning and debasing the Brisker Rav. All of this resulted in a delay in producing the placards for the religious camp and they weren't ready until erev Shabbos.*

> *Because of the late hour, the students grabbed the posters directly off the printing press and ran to show*

them to the Brisker Rav for his approval before posting them throughout the city. Reb Velvel, however, took the placards and locked them in his room. "It is erev Shabbos and winning every seat in the election isn't worth a risk of desecrating the Sabbath..." "But Rebbe, if we don't paste up our placards, the residents of Brisk will only see the posters of the irreligious and will be lured by their propaganda. We'll be careful to stop affixing the posters well before Shabbos. Please. PLEASE!!"

"Just as there is a mitzva to fight the 'Enlightenists,' likewise is there a mitzva to observe the Shabbos, and I cannot permit any risks in that regard!"

That Shabbos, Brisk was saturated with placards denouncing the religious platform and attacking the Brisker Rav — and no pro-religious posters appeared at all.

Nevertheless, it was beyond the imagination of the residents of Brisk, who had all of Shabbos to study the propaganda, what the Brisker Rav could have done to deserve such insults and ridicule. He had not posted any derisive remarks about the town's irreligious residents or their leaders. In fact, the "Enlightenist" posters appeared so unprovoked and in such poor taste that the religious camp emerged the overwhelming victors in the election — out of all proportion to their numbers.[2]

T HE SOLOVEITCHIK DYNASTY founded in Volozhin, continued in Brisk and transported to Jerusalem with Reb Velvel's immigration in 5701 (1941), hasn't lost its momentum. Three of the Brisker Rav's sons (Yosef Dov, Dovid and Meir) are the founders of three yeshivos named and patterned after the Brisker legacy. There is no one acquainted with the yeshiva world who hasn't heard of "the Brisker Yeshivos," but it wasn't always that way...

When the Brisker Rav first came to *Eretz Yisrael*, a small group of *talmidim* clustered around him. These *talmidim* heard a daily *shiur* from the Rav. In 5710 (1950) the Brisker Rav instructed his eldest son, Yosef Dov (Reb Berel) to begin delivering a *shiur*. And so, at the age of 35, nine years before the death of his father, Reb Berel became a link in the chain.

In order to encourage *talmidim* to join Reb Berel's *shiur*, the Brisker Rav spoke to his son's students periodically. Reb Berel delivered his *shiur* in the Achva Shul, situated on Reishis Chachma Street in the Geula section of Jerusalem. This shul later housed the Brisker Yeshiva.

Within the walls of this simple shul, housing bare benches and rickety *shtenders*, "Brisk" was transformed from a geographic location and elitist-didactic term into a flourishing yeshiva open to anyone who qualified. Starting with just a handful of students learning *maseches Makkos*, the Yeshiva grew to over 200 married and single *talmidim*.

T HE BURGEONING OF "BRISK" defies all norms of yeshiva expansion. It doesn't have *rebbeim*, a *mashgiach*, an executive director, fund solicitors, a dormitory, dining facilities, a secretary, a telephone, stationery, a mailbox, or even a yeshiva building. In fact, Reb Berel used to remove the foil lining from cigarette boxes and write all the daily information pertinent to the yeshiva on the back of that little paper. "This is the office," Reb Berel would say, tapping the silver scrap stuffed in his breast pocket...[3]

How could such a "yeshiva" — as inappropriate as such a term sounds in light of the above — exist, let alone thrive? The answer lies in its *Rosh Yeshiva*, his *shiur* and his mission. Reb Berel viewed himself as the authentic transmitter of the Soloveitchik-Brisker Torah. He could have spread his own wings, developed and related his own Torah thoughts — as he was so eminently capable of doing. Revealing his own genius would certainly have won him fame in the Torah world as a prominent, original *gaon* and *rosh yeshiva*. But Reb Berel chose otherwise.

While Reb Chaim's *talmidim* became the next generation's *gedolim* and *roshei yeshiva,* the Brisker Yeshiva in Jerusalem became the conduit of the Brisker legacy. Reb Chaim and the Brisker Rav would continue to deliver their *shiurim* — through their progeny. Reb Berel was a relay station: the voice was his but the ideas, concepts and methodology were those of his father and grandfather.

To assist in the perfection of the transmission, the Yeshiva's syllabus was limited to *seder Kodshim* (and *maseches Nazir*), one of the most cryptic and esoteric sections of the Talmud. *Kodshim* deals primarily with sacrifices and Temple rites. The Chofetz Chaim advocated learning *Kodshim* so that Jews will be familiar and prepared for the advent of the Messiah.

It isn't clear why the Brisker Rav specifically promoted *Kodshim* as a method by which to develop the "Brisker *derech.*" Some have suggested that the other sections of the Talmud are too thoroughly treated by the earlier and later commentaries to allow for rigorous, original and independent expression. *Kodshim,* on the other hand, is only nominally discussed.[4] Others contend that Reb Velvel's greatest proficiency was achieved in *Kodshim,* perhaps because it was this section that he studied the most under the aegis of his father.[5]

By concentrating on *Kodshim,* the Brisker Rav, via Reb Berel, highlighted its salience. The critico-conceptual method of minutely dividing and explaining every passage and opinion was applied to tractates *Zevachim, Menachos, Temurah, Bechoros* and *Nazir.* In short, Reb Chaim developed the Brisker *derech,* the Brisker Rav applied it, and Reb Beryl disseminated it by opening a yeshiva for its study.

T HERE WAS one other principle which Reb Beryl administered as unyieldingly in the Yeshiva as his forebears had in Brisk — *Emmes.** An indolent, superficial thinker was alien to the Yeshiva. *Emmes* with its exacting demands and strict specifications reigned unchallenged — without compromise or vacillation. A thought or essay which did not fit into the austere parameters of *Emmes* was invalid and rejected out of hand. Since *Emmes* is unrelenting, so must Torah study be. *Aggadata,* interpretations of Scriptural verses, *piyuttim,* etc. must all be placed under the microscope of *Emmes* and not be relegated to hermeneutics or the like. This didn't make study in the Yeshiva easy — but it did make it prestigious.

* The Brisker concept of *Emmes* is synonymous with "purity" and is not defined as "honesty" or "truth."

Brisk also demanded conformity in political outlook and personal activity, for *Emmes* cannot tolerate a partial truth, "good intentions" or an "end justifying the means." Reb Berel became the watchdog of *Emmes* in *Eretz Yisrael* and the expression "What will they say in Brisk?" has become a moral barometer.

When yeshivos and *chadorim* wished to accept Israeli government assistance and subsidies, Reb Berel intervened. If you accept their money you may fall prey to their supervision, he reasoned. A yeshiva cannot allow itself to be subject to outside influences. For this very reason his grandfather, great-grandfather and great-great-grandfather closed the doors of Volozhin.

Likewise, when the Likud came to power in 1977 and offered numerous incentives for the Agudath Israel party to join their coalition government, Reb Berel objected vehemently. Joining forces with non-religious factors was unthinkable to one schooled in the teachings of Brisk. While the Aguda party celebrated its achievements and basked in the concessions granted by the Begin government, Reb Berel looked on in disdain.

REB BERYL did not have to rely only on his lineage for the right to police *Emmes*, for he embodied the notion in pedagogy and lifestyle. His house was furnished as sparingly as the Yeshiva. It was a crowded, two-bedroom apartment with cracked, peeling walls, a crumbling floor, and a couch which consisted of protruding springs and steel bars partially covered by worn fabric. Into this cramped apartment 100 *talmidim* crowded to hear their master's *shiur*. (Four morning and three afternoon *shiurim* were delivered weekly to different groups; a *shiur* in *Zeraim* was given at night to a select group of veteran students; plus a *shiur* in *Parsha,* delivered every *Motzai Shabbos.*) The waiting list to get into *"shiur"* was usually eleven months long and was regulated by the number of people who could fit into the house.

Reb Berel saw to it that unparalleled standards of truth and honesty governed the Yeshiva. He would not accept a donation to the Yeshiva unless he could verify the purity of its source. Indeed, the slightest doubt would disqualify a contribution.

For example, he would refuse a donation from a woman unless he knew for certain that her husband consented. Anonymous donations were not accepted, and it goes without saying that money obtained illegally or from a non-observer was refused.* He had an assurance from his father that a yeshiva will succeed only if it ran on *"kosher gelt."*

When it came to distributing money, his standards were just as high. Every *Rosh Chodesh* (and never a day later), Reb Berel disbursed a modest stipend to *bochurim* (who had to tend to their own needs in the absence of yeshiva facilities) and married students. What he gave was exact.

Reb Berel had an elaborate system for calculating a person's needs. He would question a student to determine whether he received any outside assistance or if his wife was working. Did he have a refrigerator, a washing machine, etc.? In the Brisker Yeshiva, money was disbursed according to need — not scholastic ability or *yichus.*

* A recommendation from one's *rosh yeshiva* was mandatory in order to be eligible for a fellowship from the Keren Gavrilovitz fund in Tel Aviv. Once, when a Brisker student applied for the scholarship, Reb Berel investigated the source and background of the fund for over two weeks, before agreeing to write an endorsement.

One who wanted to witness the true meaning of הנותן בעין יפה ובסבר פנים יפות — giving generously and with a pleasant countenance — had to see Reb Berel distribute the money. He maintained that the person accepting the money was doing *him* the favor. "I am merely a גבאי צדקה — 'charity custodian' " — he would say to reassure anyone hesitant about receiving money from a man who barely had enough to live. Whatever money may have accumulated, he gave away and never put any aside for the coming month — his trust in God was absolute.

In honor of *Yom Tov*, he doubled the students' stipend and it was only the second portion which was occasionally late in coming. (The second portion was designated for the holiday still weeks away, otherwise it too would have been available on the first of the month — no matter what hardship that would have entailed.)

Reb Berel also arranged the support of dozens of families who never knew how their income arrived. He also paid the water, electricity and heating bills of the Achva Shul which hosted the Yeshiva.

REB BEREL was equally concerned with the spiritual and the physical needs of his students. He was a mentor *par excellence*, and would speak at length with his *talmidim* about any matter. His wisdom and perception in so many disciplines resulted in his students' seeking his counsel in every area:

> One day in the middle of a shiur a talmid came panting into the house. Reb Berel, it was known, would do anything not to miss or interrupt a shiur. But when he saw his student's frenetic state, he stood up and asked what the problem was.

> "My wife is in labor, and the doctor wants to

> *perform a Caesarean section — I don't know if I should agree..."*
>
> *Reb Berel closed his Gemara and ran arm-in-arm with his student to the hospital. Not only did he want to verify the facts for himself, but he didn't trust his student to think coherently or to instruct precisely in his condition.*
>
> *The doctor, who had mocked the idea of consulting with a rabbinic authority, changed his mind after meeting and discussing the matter with Reb Berel...*[6]

Such was the devotion Reb Berel had for his *talmidim*. He would provide them with everything — except halachic decisions. In this regard, he, like his father and many other Briskers, was an expert in avoiding *shailos* (halachic rulings). Rendering a halachic decision requires ruling in accordance with one opinion, to the exclusion of another. This is anathema to Briskers, who strive to reconcile every halachic opinion — even contradictory ones.

A S DEMANDING as Reb Berel was of his students in the realm of learning and *Emmes*, so was he when it came to *chessed*:

> *Reb Shmuel Dovid Movshovitz recommended to a friend of his from Petach Tikva that he attend the Brisker Yeshiva, and escorted him to the Rosh Yeshiva's interview. Not long after the interview began, the new student emerged alabaster-white. "Shmuel Dovid, it didn't go well and I made a fool of myself." Movshovitz pressed him for details, but he despondently left for home without revealing what had happened.*

A few minutes later Reb Berel entered the beis midrash — *a rare occurrence* — *looking for Movshovitz. "Your friend started relating his* shtikel [*Torah thought*] *and in the middle* — *I suppose out of nervousness* — *he became tongue-tied like a mute and he couldn't finish speaking."*

Three weeks later, during the Yeshiva recess, Movshovitz heard that Reb Berel was anxiously looking for him. He hurried to his Rebbe, who instructed him to fetch his friend right away so that Reb Berel could inform him personally that he had been accepted to the Yeshiva. "But he lives in Petach Tikva," protested Movshovitz.

"It doesn't matter. I discussed it with my father [*who had passed away in the interim*] *and he ordered me to accept him immediately, or the* bochur *may remain desolate for years over the incident." Movshovitz did as he was told and rushed to Petach Tikva to notify his friend.*

Reb Berel did far more than he was told. He accepted the bochur *into the Yeshiva and into his heart. Reb Berel noticed that this fellow's speech impediment had generated social problems and low self-esteem. His affection and care for this* bochur *was so great it seemed as if he considered himself responsible for the problem – all because of their initial encounter. Indeed Reb Berel personally undertook to "marry off" this student – and fulfilled his pledge...*[7]

It was very evident to Reb Berel that despite the Yeshiva's success in such minimal conditions, a permanent yeshiva building would eventually have to be sought. Indeed the Brisker Rav was the first one to finance this project by handing his son a few Pounds* earmarked for a building. Friends and supporters of the Yeshiva bought the home of the Brisker Rav and began to expand and add floors for this very purpose — but Reb Berel never lived to see the completion of this project.

HE DID LIVE to see his family's tradition carried on. He became a link in the Brisker chain that was forged with such scholarship and piety, that when it was severed Friday morning, the second of Adar Aleph 5741, the news spread pain and grief across the Torah globe. Tens of thousands of admirers and friends gathered outside that famous house on Menachem Street in Jerusalem where countless *shiurim* had been delivered in the Brisker tradition.

At the conclusion of the funeral service, Eliyahu Chaim Shapiro,[8] in the name of the students of the Brisker Yeshiva, announced that a new link had been added: Reb Berel's eldest son, Reb Avraham Yehoshua, who had already started giving *shiurim* in his father's lifetime, had been appointed the successor and *Rosh Yeshiva* of his father's Brisker Yeshiva.

* The "Pound" was the Israeli currency which preceded the Shekel.

Notes

1. *Ishim Veshitos*, Rabbi S.Y. Zevin, p. 77.
2. Rabbi Y. Galinsky.
3. His students.
4. *Ibid.*
5. His family.
6. His students.
7. *Ibid.*
8. *Hamodia*, 4 Adar I, 5741.

The Last Hundred Days
Reb Chaim Shmuelevitz

The Last Hundred Days

REB CHAIM SHMUELEVITZ *zt"l* (5663/1902-5739/1978) was the famed dean of the Mirrer Yeshiva in Jerusalem. Son-in-law of the previous Mirrer *Rosh Yeshiva,* Reb Eliezer Yehudah Finkel *zt"l,* he had already assumed a position of leadership during the yeshiva's exile in Shanghai in the World War II era. He succeeded his father-in-law in 1965, and was recognized as one of the world's greatest scholars and *roshei yeshiva.*

૭ૐ

THOSE LAST hundred days... the heart aches at the remembrance. As a flame ascends just before it burns out, so were our hopes raised at the end only to be extinguished.

When Reb Chaim, the *Rosh Yeshiva,* failed to appear on Rosh Hashanah, it was evident how ill he was. His absence was pronounced for Reb Chaim's daily presence was so conspicuous that his nonappearance was as tangible as the sudden removal of all the *shtenders* (lecterns) from the yeshiva might have been. We did not know what his ailment was; his family would tell us only to learn and say *Tehillim* for him.

ON *KOL NIDRE* night the *Rosh Yeshiva* was helped into the *beis midrash*. In his later years, Reb Chaim had never looked too well. Although his smile at the news of a *chassan,* a birth, a *chiddush,* a *yeshua* (salvation) for *Klal Yisrael* etc., could light up a room, he looked every day of his age. But on that night he looked — *Hashem yerachem!*

After resting for but a few minutes he ascended the steps adjacent to the *aron kodesh* to address the yeshiva: "Yom Kippur cannot atone until one appeases his neighbor." His eyes welled with tears as he repeated himself. We did not know it at the time, but this was his last address; he was asking for forgiveness. As he feebly descended the stairs in obvious pain he stopped and exclaimed, *"Zeht vuss ken verren fun ah mentsch"* — "Look at me! Look what can become of a man." The most powerful Yom Kippur *drasha* (speech) ever uttered in just seven words.

THE NEXT MORNING Reb Chaim was confined to bed and could not come to *davening.* At the end of *Ne'ila* there was only one thought in our minds. When we reached *Avinu Malkeinu* at the conclusion of *Ne'ila* the yeshiva was ablaze with the fervor of our prayers.

Avinu Malkeinu, our Father, our King, remember us favorably, seal us in the book of happy life, *Avinu Malkenu!* Our Father, our King, *shlach refuah sheleimah lecholei amecha* — Send a complete recovery to the sick of your nation, especially to Chaim Leib ben Ettel! The windows vibrated; the walls seemed to shake; the *tefillah* was thunderous. In Heaven it was heard; he was living on borrowed time.

ON *HOSHANAH RABBA* a man knocked on the door of the Shmuelevitz apartment to ask the *Rosh*

Yeshiva to pray on behalf of a sick person. The family refused, for Reb Chaim was already critically ill. Over their protests, however, the visitor managed to enter and presented the *Rosh Yeshiva* with a slip of paper on which the sick person's name was written. Reb Chaim recognized the name and insisted that he be taken to the *Kosel* (Western Wall) to pray for the *choleh*. The family stared incredulously at Reb Chaim. They tried to dissuade him, but as they knew only too well, trying to oppose the dictates of Reb Chaim's heart was no facile endeavor.

The *Rosh Yeshiva* had always followed the dictates of his heart; his benevolent concern for his fellow Jew was legendary. Long before, he had shepherded the yeshiva exiles in Shanghai during the war, as he did later for both foreign and local students in Jerusalem. Every *erev* Yom Kippur he would go to *Kever Rochel* and weep. "Rochel our Mother, *Hakadosh Baruch Hu* requests you to hold back your tears. The Father wants you to stop crying, but your son Chaim Leib asks you to persist. Go before His throne of glory and beg mercy for your children living in oppression..."

Despite the family's adamant refusal, a taxi was ordered to convey Reb Chaim to the Old City. He had to be helped inside, and from the taxi was literally lifted to the *Kosel*, for he no longer had any strength of his own. He uttered a fervent prayer, was carried back to the car and was returned to his bed.

WE WERE NOT privileged to see Reb Chaim during Sukkos. We danced on *Simchas Torah* without the *Rosh Yeshiva*, our exemplar of Torah. But after the *hakafos*, Reb Chaim was helped into the *beis midrash*. The song changed to *"se'uh she'arim rosheichem"* and we moved aside as if we had rehearsed his entrance a dozen times.

Reb Aryeh Finkel, the *ba'al koreh* and *ba'al tefillah* (cantor), began to read the *R'shus LeChassan Torah.*

Meir'shus haKayl hagadol, hagibor, v'hanorah... hanosenes osher vechovod v'sipharah, God who provides happiness, honor, life and splendor... His eyes began to water and his throat started to swell. Each word was muffled in tears and sobs. The words of the traditional cantillation could no longer be distinguished.

Hama'areches yamim u'mosephes gevurah — Who adds days and increases strength — each word was dissolved in tears.

U'v'chein yehi ratzon milifnei haGevurah lasais chaim vachessed va'atarah le Rabi Chaim Leib ben Rephael... Therefore let it be the will before the Almighty to provide life, kindness and splendor to Rebbe Chaim Leib ben Rephael...

The entire yeshiva was on the brink of tears.

Amod, Amod, Amod, Arise, Arise, Arise, *moreinu v'rabbeinu,* our master and our teacher, *Rav Chaim Leib Chassan HaTorah.*

His son-in-law and some married students helped him rise to his feet. Both arms supported, he was led to the Torah. This was to be Reb Chaim's last *aliyah.* He uttered each word with agonizing pain. How fitting that the *masmid* who spent every waking hour engaged in Torah study, was to hold the *Sefer Torah* for the last time as her groom!

FROM THEN on Reb Chaim's condition deteriorated drastically. *Tehillim* were recited around the clock. *"Zechus* (merit) petitions" were circulated, hoping to express the vital need Reb Chaim filled. Dozens of married students promised to attend, upon recovery, the *va'adim* and *chaburos* (various classes and lectures) the *Rosh Yeshiva* offered. One sheet, hundreds of signatures long, was a declaration to learn an extra amount every day for the *zechus* of the *Rosh Yeshiva*.

On the last day of the yeshiva recess, the 29th of *Tishrei,* Reb Chaim was admitted to Shaarei Tzedek Hospital when his illness was aggravated by a severe case of pneumonia. The doctors predicted that he would not survive the weekend. A *mishmar* (all-night study session) was called that Thursday in the yeshiva. The yeshiva *bochurim,* joined by married students who remained in the yeshiva, learned with burning diligence all night long. At 11:30 p.m. the yeshiva was as crowded as it normally is in the midst of afternoon *seder* (session). At midnight, prayers were recited, immediately followed by the resumption of learning.

On Sunday, Monday and Tuesday a *minyan* worked in shifts around the clock, learning and reciting *Tehillim* for the *Rosh Yeshiva.* In the middle of the week doctors announced that to their astonishment the pneumonia had cleared up; nevertheless, the danger not yet over. The reports we received from the hospital were far from optimistic and the situation remained critical. A grandchild overheard Reb Chaim utter *viduy;* nurses reported no improvement.

On Thursday the yeshiva *davened* the *Yom Kippur kattan* service and the *Rosh Yeshiva*'s name was changed by Reb Aryeh Finkel to *Yosef* Chaim Leib. *Repha'einu* in *chazaras hashatz* seemed endless: each word was drowned in tears and barely audible.

"Yosef Chaim Leib ben Ettel" became the focus of our prayers. Countless times the yeshiva poured down *en masse* to the *Kosel* to pray on his behalf. Our prayers were echoed around the world: each yeshiva recited *Tehillim* with the same resolve. The Mirrer Yeshiva sponsored several *kinusei his'orrerus* (arousal assemblies) for the *Rosh Yeshiva*'s recovery. At each and every one the yeshiva was filled to capacity to hear leading Torah authorities awake us to prayer. The *Gedolei Hador* issued a proclamation for a universal day of prayer devoted to Reb Chaim.

Every spiritual avenue was pursued to restore the *Rosh Yeshiva*'s health. All were keenly aware of what was at stake; we sensed the dimension of the imminent tragedy. Reb Moshe Feinstein said on the telephone that "the world rested upon Reb Chaim's shoulders."

HIS NAME actually said it all: "Chaim Leib" — the living lion. He reigned in the Torah world as a lion in his domain — until his very last day.

A week before he passed away, a relative visiting him in the hospital wished him a speedy recovery. No longer able to discern what was being said to him, Reb Chaim responded, "*Breng ah rayah*" (present a proof), assuming, typically, that he was being addressed concerning a Torah thought.

Reb Chaim, however, was the one to "bring a proof." For years, the Rambam's *halacha* in the laws of Talmud Torah has been a source of perplexity. How could the Rambam require (1:8) "even one afflicted with pain to study Torah"? Those agonizing last months when the *Rosh Yeshiva*'s life hung by a thread, his fist yet moved in concentric circles, his mouth still uttered fragments of Torah, his brain was still active... Reb Chaim was the embodiment of a "proof" for the Rambam.

We held our breath. Reb Chaim used to say that prayer has the power to ward off death. We tried. We tried to hold on to a *gadol* from the previous generation, a man who had mastered Torah in its entirety in both depth and clarity. There should be words to express his greatness, but we lack them.

We could not hold on. We stormed the Gates of Heaven, but apparently we were undeserving. As the last of the Chanukah candles sputtered out on the evening of the third of *Teves, Klal Yisrael*'s glowing beacon also ceased to radiate.

THE FOLLOWING morning there was a funeral of unprecedented proportion in the annals of *Klal Yisrael*. Everyone seemed to be there, *chassidim, misnagdim,* from Torah giants to simple carpenters whose shops border the Mirrer Yeshiva. Almost a hundred thousand mourners stood outside the yeshiva under the brilliant December sun while eulogies were delivered. Local bus service was suspended; the police didn't even try to contain the crowds. After the last eulogy, a human chain began to uncoil, sprawling over the entire breadth of Jerusalem. Just as the tail of the procession was leaving the Mirrer Yeshiva, the head of the *levayah* (funeral procession) arrived at *Har HaMenuchos* (the cemetery). The religious neighborhoods were like ghost towns; every shop was closed and the streets deserted.

The *talmidim* began to trickle back to the yeshiva in the early evening. Glass panes in the halls had been smashed by the tremendous crush of the crowds. Our clothes were rent as is required for the passing of a close relative. The *paroches* (ark curtain) was returned to the *aron kodesh* (ark) and benches were slowly replaced in preparation for the eulogies which would take place during the next six nights.

Thousands came to console the Shmuelevitz family during the week of *shiva* (mourning). Previously unknown stories of the *Rosh Yeshiva*'s greatness began to circulate, tales so amazing that they were hard to believe but easy to inspire — things we cannot hope to achieve, but for which we can yearn and strive.

The Vision of
Yechezkel

Reb Yechezkel Abramsky

The Vision of
Yechezkel

RABBI YECHEZKEL ABRAMSKY *zt"l* used to say that a person's life is like a book: the day of birth is the first page; the day of death, the last page. Each intermediate day is a separate page in the book that man is assigned to author. Reb Yechezkel (Chatzkal) Abramsky, who was born on 5 Adar, 5646 (1886), in the small town of Dashkovtse, near the Mosst district of Vilna, wrote a wondrous work that was 90 years long.

WHEN REB YECHEZKEL was only eight years old, he could quote entire chapters from *Tanach* by heart, to the delight of the Jews of Mosst. At seventeen, he left home to learn in Novardhok under the *"Alter"* — Rabbi Yosef Yoizel Horowitz. In less than a year, he received *smicha* from the Rav of Novardhok, Rabbi Yechiel Michal Epstein, author of the *Aruch Hashulchan.*

Reb Yechezkel left Novardhok to study in the Telshe yeshiva. Due to the unsuccessful revolution in Russia and the infamous army conscription, Telshe became isolated from the yeshiva world. Food was scarce and the yeshiva's only *sefarim* were *gemaras* and the *Chiddushei HaRashba.* Reb Yechezkel mastered them all.

His diligence was renowned even before his arrival in Telshe. He used to say that a *masmid,* a diligent student, is one who learns sixty minutes an hour. When his sister passed away, he told a group of *talmidei chachamim* who had come to console him of Reb Chaim Soloveitchik's explanation of the *Yerushalmi Moed Kattan:* "A mourner who is adamant that he learn Torah may do so during the period of mourning when Torah study is forbidden." A mourner is not permitted to study Torah because of the prohibition against joy, which study promotes. A mourner, however, is not required to inflict pain on himself. Therefore, one who is so obsessed with Torah study and actually aches in its absence, would be permitted to resume his study. The *talmidei chachamim* immediately told Reb Yechezkel that he may resume studying.

When Reb Yechezkel reached conscription age for the Czarist army, he was forced to leave Telshe for Vilna, the "Jerusalem of Lithuania." There he entered the Ramalies Yeshiva and became acquainted with Reb Chanoch Aigesh, author of the *Marcheshes.* Rav Aigesh was greatly impressed with the young Yechezkel Abramsky — so impressed that he recommended to his cousin, Rabbi Yisrael Yehonason Yerushalemsky, that he consider Reb Yechezkel as a suitable match for his daughter. And so, on *erev Rosh Chodesh* Tammuz, 5669 (1909), the couple were married in Eihuman.

AFTER REB YECHEZKEL HAD LIVED in the home of his father-in-law for a year and a half, Rav Yerushalemsky advised him to continue his studies under the famed Reb Chaim "Brisker" Soloveitchik. Reb Yechezkel followed the advice, and spent four months with Reb Chaim. It was an encounter which marked the start of a long and fruitful relationship, one that found expression in many areas, including Reb Yechezkel's own commentary on *Chiddushei Rabbeinu Chaim Halevy al HaRambam.*

Reb Yechezkel considered Reb Chaim's words of Torah to be definitive and always deferred to him in any dispute. He once related that after he had written a *chiddush* on the *Tosephta,* Reb Chaim appeared to him in a dream and urged, *"Min darf lernen mehr Torah"* (One must learn more Torah). As soon as he awoke, he reviewed his notes and found that the very *mishna* he had intended to use as a proof in support of his argument, in fact served as a refutation of it.

THE LUBAVITCHER REBBE, Rabbi Shalom Ber, invited Reb Yechezkel to be the *Rosh Yeshiva* of his Tomchei Temimim Yeshiva. The students were so enthralled by his lectures that they lingered long after the classes were over to discuss his ideas further. This resulted in their late arrival for the daily *Tanya* class. When the Lubavitcher Rebbe learned of this, he informed Reb Yechezkel that while his greatness in Torah was genuinely admired, he would be better suited to direct a different yeshiva.

The Rebbe advised the Chabad chassidim of Smolian to accept Reb Yechezkel as their Rabbi. On his second day in Smolian, he was asked his first *shailah* (halakhic query) — and for some reason he could not remember the ruling. This was a significant test for him as his reputation was at stake. He could easily have replied in an ambiguous manner, but his honesty compelled him to respond: "I don't know."*

* On one hot *shiva assar beTammuz* fast day, a man knocked on Reb Yechezkel's door to solicit charity for his daughter's wedding. Reb Yechezkel gave him his usual donation and later that evening found the

In 5674 (1914), Reb Yechezkel accepted the invitation to succeed Rabbi Avraham Duber Kahane (author of *Dvar Avraham*) as head of the prestigious community of Smolovitch. With the outbreak of World War I that year, Rabbi Chaim Brisker resettled in Minsk, a half-hour's train ride from Smolovitch. Reb Yechezkel adopted the custom of leaving Smolovitch for Minsk every Sunday and returning in time for Shabbos. For three consecutive years these trips continued and profoundly affected Reb Yechezkel's development as a *talmid chacham* and leader of *Klal Yisrael*.

REB YECHEZKEL never discussed his plans to embark on writing his monumental work on the *Tosephta* (writings parallel to the *Mishna* under the redaction of Rav Hiyya and Rav Oshiya), the *Chazon Yechezkel*, with his rebbe. Nevertheless, one day Reb Chaim overheard Reb Yechezkel discuss a complex subject related to the *Tosephta* with Reb Chaim's son, Velvel (the Brisker Rav). "It is apparent from your words," he said, "that you intend to write a book on the *Tosephta* — a most necessary project." To Reb Yechezkel these words implied his rebbe's approval for what was to become his life's occupation.

[When his wife became ill, Reb Yechezkel contemplated delaying the publication of some of his manuscripts until a time when he was less anxious and could concentrate completely on his work. Reb Yechezkel employed the *Goral HaGra* to solve his dilemma, and when the *goral*

---

same man in the synagogue. Reb Yechezkel invited him to break the fast at his house, which was close by, and save walking back in the heat on an empty stomach. The offer was declined with the confession: "I didn't fast." When Reb Yechezkel heard this, he contributed even more money, saying, "Now I see that you are truly an honest man."

landed on the verse, "*Yizal mayim medalyo*" — water shall
flow from His bucket (Bamidbar 24:7), he understood that
publication should proceed as planned.]

The importance Reb Yechezkel attached to the *Chazon
Yechezkel* is clear from his *tzava'a* (will), in which he
instructed that his books be borne behind him at his
funeral. He also promised to be an advocate in the
Heavenly Court for anyone who studied from his books.
Reb Yechezkel's intention was to introduce the *Tosephta*
into the yeshiva curriculum: "Each and every *halacha*
should be explained in a simple and clear manner according
to the literal meaning of the words, rejecting any
interpretations foreign to *halacha* and incompatible with
what is written." (From the introduction to *Zeraim*.)

Despite the fact that the *Tosephta* is one of the primary
sources for both Talmuds — *Yerushalmi* and *Bavli* — the
Tosephta had never attained any popularity in yeshivos.
The *Chazon Yechezkel* brought the *Tosephta* out of the
crypt with a *bayur,* a terse explanation of the *Tosephta*'s
words, and *chiddushim,* explanations of the *Tosephta* in
light of the *gemara* and *Rishonim.*

A T THE END of World War I, the Jews continued to
suffer persecution. In Smolovitch, where Reb
Yechezkel was the Rabbi, the anti-Semitic Poles perpetrated countless atrocities, including the shaving off of
Jews' beards by force. When the thugs arrived at Reb
Yechezkel's house he exclaimed, "I am a Rabbi and a Rabbi
must have a beard!" His bold response startled his
assailants and they decided to leave him alone. Reb
Yechezkel, however, was not content until he received an
official document from the authorities prohibiting the
removal of his beard. This heroic story quickly spread

among the Jews and inspired countless others not to succumb to the ruthless intruders.

Following the Bolshevik Revolution in 1917, the position of the Jews in Russia deteriorated considerably. Even religious marriage was banned. Despite the great danger involved, when Rabbi Abramsky heard of a bride and groom who wished to be wed, he would invite them to his house where he would marry them in secret.

WHEN RABBI Issar Zalman Meltzer left Russia in 5683 (1923), the Jews of Slutzk asked Reb Yechezkel to replace him as their Rabbi. He served as the Rabbi of Slutzk, displaying great self-sacrifice for nearly seven years. Reb Yechezkel ensured that the sacred covenant of circumcision remained alive, and regularly gave part of his meager salary to the *mohel* in nearby Harazuva.*

Whenever a male child was born, Reb Yechezkel would visit the family and plead with them to have the baby circumcised, despite the danger. To facilitate this, he devised the following plan: The father would leave his house on the day of the *bris.* Rebbetzen Abramsky, laden with baskets from the market, would stop in front of the baby's house and remove her shoe. This was a sign to the *mohel,* following close behind, to enter and quickly perform the sacred ritual.

While in Slutzk, Reb Yechezkel joined with Rabbi Shlomo Yosef Zevin in publishing a Torah journal, *Yigdal*

---

* During his stay in Smolovitch, he donated a large portion of his salary to hire a man to discreetly inform the local Jews every *erev Shabbos* before sundown that, "The Shabbos Queen is approaching; it is time to close your shops."

Torah, which was outlawed by the Communist government after just two issues were published.

Reb Yechezkel was also a member of a rabbinical council partially sponsored by the Lubavitcher Rebbe, Rabbi Yosef Yitzhak Schneerson, dedicated to strengthening Jewish observance in Russia. The Soviet authorities considered Reb Yechezkel's membership in the council subversive and warned him repeatedly to stop all activities related to the council. They also refused to allow him to leave Russia in order to accept an invitation to become the Rabbi of Petach Tikva, after the passing of Reb Yisrael Abba Citron. From that moment on, Reb Yechezkel was in constant danger.*

AFTER TEN MONTHS of hiding — moving to Moscow, Leningrad and other places — he was apprehended on *erev Rosh Chodesh* Elul 5690 (1930). He was accused of trying to overthrow the Soviet regime and was imprisoned in Moscow's infamous Lubyanka prison. The accusation was based on his meeting with Rabbi Yeshaya Glazer, a member of a United States fact-finding mission, which was investigating the state of religious freedom in the Soviet Union. Several months earlier, fourteen leading rabbis had been arrested in Minsk on the same charge after meeting with Rabbi Glazer. Despite the fact that Reb Yechezkel did not utter a word during his meeting with Glazer, the prosecutor demanded the death penalty. Owing to outside pressure, the sentence was commuted to five years of hard labor in Siberia.

From the time of his arrest, Reb Yechezkel's life became

* Reb Yechezkel once left his congregation on *Hoshana Rabba* in order to spend *Shmini Atzeres* and *Simchas Torah* together with Rabbi Zevin. He confided to his host that he felt the "earth burning under his feet."

a nightmare. He suffered terrible tortures in the cellars of the secret police: "At first they tried to persuade me to confess and be absolved from punishment. When they saw that this was to no avail, they said that they had ways of eliciting confessions that no human could endure. I realized that they didn't want only my soul, but the souls of all the rabbis. I therefore declared: 'I do not doubt your ability to harm me. I know that you can cut out my tongue and chop off my hands if you wish, but you will never succeed in getting me to utter a falsehood or sign an untrue statement.'"

REB YECHEZKEL arrived in Siberia wearing lightweight clothing which was virtually useless in that climate. "Every morning," he once related, "in temperature that often plummeted to 40 degrees below zero, we were forced to take off our shoes and run barefoot in the snow. From this torture alone, men fell like flies. I looked toward heaven and cried, 'Master of the Universe, you have taught us that everything is in the hands of Heaven except cold and heat (*Kesubos* 30a). Cold and heat are in man's own hands since man can guard himself from the elements by donning a coat or removing a sweater. This reason, however, no longer applies to me, for these iniquitous captors not only fail to provide me with clothes but force me to remove whatever I am wearing. My obligation to guard my health, therefore, returns to You. So please protect me, O God, for I trust in You!'

"As a child," he continued, "my mother always bundled me up warmly due to my frailty, while in the midst of that freezing Siberian cold I never once took ill or even caught a cold!"

Reb Yechezkel's first job was sawing heavy logs. When he was unable to fill his quota, he was punished with the assignment of stringing frozen fish onto wire. It was a dangerous task: he could not string the fish without wearing gloves, but with gloves on he couldn't feel the needle or the wire. Enervated, he uttered the "*viduy*" confessional every time he held the wire in his hand. After several weeks he was transferred to the more monotonous but less hazardous job of slicing bread for all the prisoners.

Reb Yechezkel once related that for a time he found it difficult to say the *Modeh Ani* prayer. "Why should I thank the Almighty for 'restoring my soul within me' for another torturous day? What kindness is there in mercifully restoring my soul if I cannot worship You properly? Until I finally realized that '*rabba emunasecha*' — Thy faithfulness is great! I thank You for providing me with an additional day of faith — it is worth enduring all these tortures as long as I can continue living and having faith in God for an extra moment."

ALMOST ALL of the twenty-four volume *Chazon Yechezkel* was written when Reb Yechezkel was a destitute prisoner. Rabbi Zevin testified that the words of the *Tosephta* never left Reb Yechezkel's lips, even when he was slaving at the most strenuous labor. Reb Yechezkel wrote in the introduction to *Zeraim* that even during the difficult days of World War I and in the subsequent years under Bolshevik oppression, "I did not cease to study and delve into the words of the *Tosephta*. While mountains were humbled with fear of the enemy and the Torah deserters raged like the tempest, I found the study of the *Tosephta* to be my greatest delight."*

* Prior to Reb Yechezkel's incarceration in Siberia, he had the foresight to entrust the *Chazon Yechezkel* manuscripts to Michael Rabinowitz, who brought the work with him to *Eretz Yisrael*. The manuscripts were later forwarded to a relative of Reb Yechezkel's, Reb Alter Vernofsky, who published the first volumes together with an introduction which

A good portion of his novellae were written on the scraps of paper rationed out to prisoners for rolling cigarettes and without the aid of references. Reb Yechezkel's happiest day throughout the terrible ordeal was the day the authorities allowed his wife to bring him a volume of the *Tosephta*. And whenever he managed to send a letter to one of his colleagues, he did not describe the tortures he was suffering — instead, he invariably wrote something related to the *Tosephta*.

Reb Yechezkel's imprisonment in Siberia sparked an outcry in the Jewish world to secure his release. On *erev Yom Kippur* 5692 (1931), he was finally freed.*

During Reb Yechezkel's incarceration in Siberia, Europe's leading rabbis added the name "Yosef" to Yechezkel in the hope that he would merit release, just as *Yosef Hatzaddik* was saved from the Egyptian prison. Reb Yechezkel always cited the verse, "Then Pharoah sent and called Joseph and they brought him hastily out of the dungeon," when discussing his release. According to the interpretation of the Sforno, "Every Divine salvation is done in an instant." When Reb Yechezkel was finally freed on *erev* Yom Kippur, he didn't even have time to tie his shoelaces.

After his release, Reb Elchonon Wasserman greeted him and related the following story: "That very *erev* Yom Kippur I was learning with the Chofetz Chayim when all of a

---

alluded to the Iron Curtain separating the work from its author. When Reb Yechezkel was freed from Siberia in 5692 (1931), and settled in London, the other volumes were finally published.

* Reb Yechezkel's deliverance from Siberia was the result of tireless efforts of the *Gedolei Hador* and the unprecedented intervention of the German Counselor, H. Bruening, who arranged the release in exchange for six communists jailed in Germany.

sudden he exclaimed, 'The Bolsheviks did not succeed, the Bolsheviks did not succeed! They were forced to free the Rav of Slutzk' — and then the Chofetz Chayim resumed learning. I looked at the clock and later found out to my astonishment that you were freed at that very hour!"

IN 5692 (1931), Reb Yechezkel was appointed Rabbi of the Machzikei Hadass Synagogue in London. After serving for two years as Rabbi, he was invited by the United Synagogues to head the Central *Beis Din* of Great Britain. This *Beis Din* was the fountainhead of the British Jewish communities. Reb Yechezkel made his acceptance of the post contingent upon stipulations regarding conversions and standards of *kashrus.* When these conditions were finally met — after a year and a half of negotiations — he accepted the post.

A London butcher who opposed Rabbi Abramsky's new *kashrus* standards lodged an appeal in court, claiming that the edicts did not conform with the spirit of freedom and democracy in Britain. When Rabbi Abramsky was subpoenaed to appear in court to answer the claim, community leaders, familiar with his strong will and his outspokenness, beseeched him not to agitate the stately and composed British judges. Unimpressed, Reb Yechezkel entered the courtroom and declared in a raised voice, "Nothing can stand before the truth! Democracy was created to protect and serve the truth and cannot be relieved of this obligation. When a Jew orders kosher meat he means exclusively meat that a knowledgeable Torah authority has certified, and anything other than that is fraud. The man who has come to protest this simple truth has sinned twice over: he denies the foundation of truth and degrades democracy as if it were made to serve lies..." In his judgement, the judge noted that, "albeit this old tiger roared a roar this courtroom is not used to hearing, I must, nevertheless, unequivocally rule that he is correct."

Despite Reb Yechezkel's forceful nature, he was able to endure insults and accept abuse when necessary. During the period of World War II, a man whose allegiance to Judaism was, at best, tenuous, began beating his wife and refused to agree to a divorce. In order to guarantee his wife's misfortune and destine her to become an *agunah,* he converted to Catholicism. Reb Yechezkel, always anxious to save a Jewish daughter from misfortune, offered to speak to the convert.

The *meshumad* finally acquiesced. He agreed to grant his wife a divorce, but not before he had hurled a volley of insults at the Rabbi and all Jews. After the *get* was delivered, the convert told his former wife to remain behind for he wished to settle some financial matters with her.

Had she remained behind, it would have violated the Rambam's opinion of *veshilchah* — that the woman must be sent out of the house. Reb Yechezkel ruled that if she remained behind it would invalidate the *get,* which had been obtained with such difficulty. The *meshumad* was incensed and he let loose a fresh barrage of insults and curses at Reb Yechezkel and the Jewish people in general. Nevertheless, Reb Yechezkel controlled his anger beyond the point of Hillelian tolerance and remained silent but firm until his *psak* was upheld. He later commented to his son that he was glad that he had remembered this Rambam when it was *halacha lema'aseh* and not just for his writings.

REB YECHEZKEL took his communal responsibility seriously. His son related that he always stood behind his father on the *Yomim Noraim* in order to help him rise after he had gone down on his knees for *Kor'im.* One year during *Kor'im* Reb Yechezkel began to cry. "What was it that you were praying for," his son asked, assuming that Reb Yechezkel must be praying for success in Torah learning, for health and for sustenance, or perhaps that his sons should be *talmidei chachamim.* To his son's surprise, Reb Yechezkel replied: "I am praying that all the matzos baked under my supervision should be truly free of any *chometz.*" Years later, after moving to Israel, he confided that when he went down on his knees during *Kor'im,* he then prayed that the *Chinuch Atzmai* school systems should never lose their financial backing.

Reb Yechezkel's son also described how, during World War II, his father pressured a Jewish soldier to write a conditional *get* for his wife before he set out for combat. That way, if he failed to return, the *get* could be presented and his wife would be spared the tragedy of becoming an *agunah.* The soldier finally agreed, but only on condition that the *get* be delivered via a third party. Reb Yechezkel acquiesced and put the *get* in the safe of the London *Beis Din.* That night, London was mercilessly bombed by the Germans, and the *Beis Din* was extensively damaged. Two floors of the building were razed by the Civil Guard so that passersby would not be injured by the bombed-out, crumbling structure. Reb Yechezkel acquired a permit from the police and climbed a perilous 50-rung ladder to retrieve the *get,* so that he would be able to fulfill his guarantee to the soldier.

A poor woman once came to Reb Yechezkel with a *shailah* about a chicken. Reb Yechezkel determined that the chicken was not kosher and took ten shillings out of his pocket, saying, "The chicken cannot be eaten — here is ten shillings." The woman refused the money until he raised his voice: "I am a Rav. I ruled that the chicken is *treif* and you accepted my ruling. I also rule that you must accept the money!"

ASIDE FROM his *Beis Din* activities, Reb Yechezkel gave countless *shiurim* for hundreds of people. His devotion to *emmes*, truth, would never permit him to veer from the topic or relate any anecdotes during a Talmudic discourse.

Once when he was invited to address a *siyum* with the traditional *hadran* — that is, connecting the conclusion of the Talmud with its beginning — Reb Yechezkel rose to speak and, to the chagrin of his audience, informed them that he would not say a *hadran* but rather clarify a certain halacha. When he saw their disappointment he related the following *Chazal:* "The Rabbis say that the Leviathan spans the entire breadth of the ocean so that his tail touches his mouth — thus connecting his beginning with his end. But, say *Chazal,* he is only playing, as it says, 'The Leviathan you have created to play with.' I, however, am searching for the truth and not to play!"*

On another occasion, while examining one of his *sefarim,* Reb Yechezkel sighed and said that each time he looked at this volume his heart ached. In it he quoted one of the *Gedolei Achronim,* who deduced the opposite of a well-known *Tosephos.* "I am certain that this *gadol* knew this *Tosephos,* but it probably slipped his mind for the moment. Did I really have to publicize that he temporarily forgot a *Tosephos?*"

* Rabbi Abramsky gave a weekly class to students and *baalei battim* on the Torah portion. When they arrived at *Parshas Ki Saitzai,* he pondered how he would explain the topic of *Yif'as To'ar* (the beautiful woman captive the Torah allows one to marry) without generating a barrage of unbidden questions. As usual, he prayed to Hashem for inspiration and was blessed with an idea typical of the approach he often adopted: he started the class by saying, "The Torah descended to the very depths of man's knowledge, and permitted a trial of endurance that would be difficult to sustain; it is evident, however, that all other prohibitions underwent the same scrutiny and God determined that man can certainly stand up to them."

The London *Beis Din* published several booklets based upon *shailos* that were asked of Reb Yechezkel, along with *Dinei Mamanos* and *Eretz Yisrael Nachlas Am Yisrael.* He also published several volumes of the *Tosephta* independently.

Reb Yechezkel personally gave generously to a number of causes — especially yeshivos. When a certain *gadol* described his yeshiva's financial crisis, Reb Yechezkel immediately approached a wealthy Jew and sought his support. The man agreed to donate the entire sum needed, on condition that Reb Yechezkel would explain the words of the *Chazal*, "*Gadol hama'aseh min ha'oseh*" — he who petitions the doer is greater than the one who actually performs the deed.

"After all," said the rich man, "why should the Rabbi's reward be greater than mine? It is I who am donating the money!" Reb Yechezkel replied: "When I knocked on your door, I was so nervous I could hear my heart thump. You did not have to experience this fear... overcoming this trepidation is worth far more than the sum that you are donating."

IN 5711 (1951), when Reb Yechezkel made *aliyah,* the Torah giants of *Eretz Yisrael* gathered to greet him and many asked him to head their yeshivos. He chose to lecture at the Slabodka Yeshiva in Bnei Brak, which was under the leadership of Rabbi Yitzchak Isaac Sherr, the son-in-law of the "*Alter*" of Slabodka. For close to twenty-five years, he travelled from Jerusalem to Bnei Brak to deliver his famous *shiurim.* He used to say that he felt like a millionaire who owned two apartments, for he viewed the yeshiva in Bnei Brak as his second home.

The aim of his *shiurim* was to fulfill the commandment to

teach Torah. Keeping this intention in mind while delivering the *shiur,* he said, was harder than both the preparation and the actual delivery of the *shiur.*

He provided his students with a *derech* — an approach to learning Talmud. He never understood the desire yeshiva students have to produce their own innovative and original interpretations. "When I am able to learn a page of *gemara* without any questions, I am a happy man," he said. "By contrast, when a yeshiva student doesn't find any questions, he is terribly disappointed."

Reb Yechezkel reviewed a passage of *gemara* eight times before he delved into the underpinnings of its meaning. He said that he would be embarrassed to ever appear before one of his teachers if he had forgotten one of their lessons: "They teach and I forget? Whatever they taught is guarded within me as if it were locked in a safe!"

In addition to excellence in learning, Reb Yechezkel taught his students *middos* — good character traits — and *emunah* — faith in God — in which he himself had achieved such excellence. In addition, Rabbi Abramsky also gave a weekly *shiur* for hundreds of residents of his Jerusalem neighborhood, Bayit Vegan.

AFTER THE Six Day War, a tourist in Bayit Vegan asked him to explain the miracles which occurred during the war. Reb Yechezkel replied with a quotation from Psalms: "As the mountains surround Jerusalem, so does the Lord surround his people." He pointed to the mountains in the distance and said, "Just as these are a physical reality, likewise, God's surrounding and protecting His nation now and forevermore is a reality. That was proven in this war..."

When his eldest son, Rabbi Moshe Abramsky, died (two

years before his own death), Reb Yechezkel said the words of Psalm 119 about himself: "I have chosen the way of truth, Thy judgements have I laid before me." For the one who grasps the way of faith, everything is fair — God's attribute of justice is just like God's attribute of mercy.

At a time when it appeared that the army would draft yeshiva students, Shimon Peres, the Minister of Defense at the time, made an appointment with Reb Yechezkel, who was the head of the *Va'ad Hayeshivos,* and other *roshei yeshiva.* Rabbi Abramsky asked Mr. Peres for permission to begin with the very words with which he wished to conclude. Mr. Peres nodded his head. Rabbi Abramsky's face grew solemn as he said: "We wish to tell you that the subject is not a matter for discussion. The yeshivos are the home of life, and the Torah is the core of life, and one is not permitted to sever a life source!"

Mr. Peres turned over his briefing paper with his plan and suggestions as if to say, "I yield."

A T THE AGE of eighty-four, Reb Yechezkel suffered a heart attack and was not allowed to deliver any *shiurim,* a decree which pained him far more than the attack itself. After his recuperation, he was inspired to resume his *shiurim* by the visit of a student who demonstrated that he remembered Rabbi Abramsky's every word. The very next Shabbos the dining room of Yeshivas Kol Torah in Bayit Vegan was packed for the long-awaited *shiur.* When Reb Yechezkel arrived at the *gemara* which interprets Psalm 92 *Mizmor Shir Leyom HaShabbos,* he explained the entire chapter verse by verse:

"Planted in the house of the Lord, they shall flourish in the courts of our God." He pointed to an inconsistency in the grammar of the two words "planted" and "flourish," which occur in two different tenses. The explanation he suggested is that when a *tzaddik* leaves this world, he is already planted in the world-to-come; however, his influence here continues to increase after his death — thus flourishes, in the present tense — through his influence over the many who follow his path.

How appropriate are these words to Reb Yechezkel himself. On that *motzei* Shabbos, Elul 24, 5736 (1976), Reb Yechezkel Abramsky was invited to the Divine Court after serving God and His people through His Torah for over ninety years. His Torah teachings, however, continue to flourish.

In his great humility, he requested that in place of eulogies, it be announced at his funeral that he asks everyone for forgiveness and that he forgives everyone.

Glossary

Glossary

The following glossary provides a partial explanation of some of the foreign words and phrases used in this book. The spelling, tense, and explanations reflect the way the specific word is used in *Sunset*. Often, there are alternate spellings and meanings for the words. Foreign words and phrases which are immediately followed by a translation in the text are not included in this section.

ACHARON (ACHARONIM) — talmudic scholars of the last five hundred years

AGUNAH (AGUNOS) — lit. a "chained woman"; refers to a woman whose marriage has been terminated *de facto* but not *de jure,* and is therefore unable to remarry because she is still technically married to her absent husband

ALIYAH — going up; term used in connection with 1. being called up to the reading of the Torah; 2. immigration to Israel

ALMANAH —widow

AVINU MALKEINU — our Father our King

AVRECH — young married yeshiva student

BAALEI BATTIM — lay individuals

BAAL KOREH — reader of the Torah

BAAL MUM — individual who is halakhically blemished

BAAL TEFILLAH — leader of prayer

BAMIDBAR — Book of Numbers

BARUCH HASHEM — lit. the Lord is blessed; thank God

BEDAVKA — this specifically

BEIS DIN — court of Jewish law

BEIS HAMUSSAR — house or room devoted to the study of ethics

BEIS MIDRASH — house of study used for both Torah study and prayer

BEN BAYIS — lit. son of the house; regular guest; a virtual member of the family

BITUL TORAH — wasting time from Torah study

BNEI TORAH — lit. sons of Torah; men imbued with Torah teaching and values

BOCHUR (BOCHURIM) — unmarried yeshiva student

BREISHIS — book of Genesis

BRIS — the Jewish rite of circumcision

CHALILAH — God forbid

CHASSAN — groom

CHASSANAH — wedding

CHAZAL — 1. acronym of our sages, of blessed memory; 2. a statement by the sages

CHAZARAS HASHATZ — cantor's repetition of the main prayer

CHEVRUSA — study partner

CHIDDUSH (CHIDDUSHIM) — novellae; new insights in Torah interpretation

CHIDDUSHEI TORAH — (pl.) same as above

CHINUCH — education

CHINUCH YELADIM — education of children

CHOL HAMOED — the Intermediate Days of SUKKOS and PESACH

CHOMETZ — leaven which results when either wheat, barley, spelt, rye, or oats remain in contact with water for a period of time before baking; the Torah forbids eating or deriving any benefit from *chometz* on Passover.

CHUPAH — 1. wedding canopy; 2. the wedding service

CHURBAN — destruction; devastation caused by the Nazis ימ"ש.

COHAIN — male descendant from the priestly family of Aaron.

DAF SHIUR — GEMARA lesson focussed on the page being studied

DAVEN — (Yid.) pray

DAYAN — rabbinical court judge

DERECH — method of study

DERECH ERETZ — proper behavior or manners

DINEI TORAH — (pl.) cases brought for adjudication according to Jewish law

DIVREI TORAH — Torah thoughts

DRASHA — learned discourse

EMMES — absolute truth

ERETZ YISRAEL — the Land of Israel

EREV — eve

FLEISH — meat

GADOL HADOR — lit. great one of the generation; refers to the preeminent giant in Torah scholarship of his generation

GAON — lit. brilliant one; honorific for a distinguished sage

GEDOLEI YISRAEL — (pl.) giants in Torah scholarship

GEDOLIM — (pl.) same as above

GELT — (Yid.) money

GEMACH — contraction of *gemilus chassadim;* interest-free loan society

GEMARA — 1. commentary on the Mishna (together they compromise the Talmud); 2. a volume of the Talmud

GITTIN — (pl.) divorce documents

HACHNASSAS ORCHIM — hospitality

HAKADOSH BARUCH HU — the Holy One, blessed be He

HAKAFOS — seven joyous revolutions made around and with the Torah scrolls on the holiday of SIMCHAS TORAH

HALACHA — Jewish law

HALACHA LEMA'ASEH — practical application of Jewish law

HAMELECH — The King

HAMOTZI — the blessing made over bread

HAREI AT — opening words of wedding formula said by the groom to his bride

HAR HAZEISIM — Mount of Olives; major Jerusalem cemetery overlooking the Temple Mount

HASMADA — diligence

HESPED — eulogy

HETER — halakhic dispensation

ICH HAB A NEISS — (Yid.) I have a novel idea

ILLUI — genius; towering Torah scholar

ISH SHALOM — man of peace

KALLAH — bride

KEHILLA — organized community; congregation

KIDDUSH — sanctification; prayer recited over wine to usher in the Sabbath and festivals

KIDDUSHIN — marriage ceremony

KINYAN — act of acquisition

KIRUV — outreach efforts which attempt to acquaint assimilated Jews with their religion

KLAL YISRAEL — community of Israel; all Jewry

KNESSIAH HAGEDOLAH — lit. the great assembly; meetings convened infrequently by the great Rabbis of the generation

KOLLEL — post-graduate yeshiva, the student body of which is usually comprised of young married students who receive stipends

KORIM — the section of the *Aleinu* prayer where, on Rosh Hashanah and Yom Kippur, one goes down on one's knees

KOSEL — lit. wall; last remaining wall of the Temple courtyard, an eminent holy site

LAG B'OMER — the thirty-third day of the counting of the Omer (days between the second day of Passover and Shavuos), and also the anniversary of the death of Rabbi Shimon bar Yochai; on this day Jews may interrupt the mourning observed during the Omer

LE'ILLUI NISHMASO — in order to elevate the soul

LEVAYA — funeral

LIMUD — learning

MA'ASEH RAV — lesson derived from a scholar's behavior

MACHLOKES — dispute; polemic

MAGGID SHIUR — Talmud instructor

MAOS CHITTIM — lit. money for wheat; charity given expressly to offset the expenses of Passover necessities

MASHGIACH — dean of students in a yeshiva who acts as a spiritual guide and advisor

MASHIACH — Messiah

MECHADEISH — the act of creating a CHIDDUSH

MESHULACH — lit. messenger; itinerant fundraiser for a charitable institution

MESHUMAD — convert from Judaism

MESIRUS NEFESH — self-sacrifice

MEVAKER CHOLEH — visit the infirm

MIDDOS — character traits

MIKVEH — a ritual bath used for the purpose of ritual purification

MILAH — circumcision

MISHKAN — the Tabernacle

MISHNA(YOS) — the earliest codification of Jewish oral law by Rabbi Yehudah HaNassi

MISNAGDIM — (pl.) opposers of the Chassidic Movement

MISPALLELIM — (pl.) worshippers

MODEH ANI — lit. I render thanks; prayer said upon rising in the morning

MOSHE RABBEINU — Moses, our teacher

MUSSAR — 1. school of thought emphasizing ethical performance; 2. moral teachings; 3. ethical lecture

NAANUIM — movements of the *lulav* during the prayer service of SUKKOS

NACHAS — joy and pleasure

NAIGEL VASSER — lit. finger water; water used in the morning to wash off the impurity obtained through sleep

NEFESH — soul

NE'ILA — final additional prayer of Yom Kippur

NESHAMAH — soul

NETILAS YADAYIM — ritual washing of the hands

PEIRUSH — commentary

PEREK — chapter

PESACH — Passover

PISKEI HALACHA — halakhic rulings

PSAK — halakhic decision

PSHAT — simple interpretation; meaning

RABBANIM — Rabbis

RABBEINU — our teacher

REBBE (REBBEIM) — 1. rabbi, usually a Talmud teacher; 2. instructor; 3. chassidic leader

REBBE MUVHAK — pimary teacher

REBBETZEN — wife of a rabbi

REFU'AH SHELEIMAH — a complete recovery

RISHONIM — lit. first ones; European scholars of the eleventh through fifteenth centuries

ROSH CHODESH — beginning of the month

ROSH KEHILLA — head of the community

ROSH YESHIVA — yeshiva dean

RUACH HAKODESH — Divine spirit

SANHEDRIN — the highest judicial and ecclesiastical court of the Jewish nation

SEDER — study session in a yeshiva

SEFER (SEFARIM) — book of religious content

SHAATNEZ — forbidden mixture of wool and linen

SHABBOS (SHABBOSIM) — Sabbath

SHABBOS HAGADOL — lit. The Great Shabbos; the Sabbath preceding the Passover holiday; usually marked by a scholarly lecture-sermon of long duration, germane to the holiday

SHACHARIS — the morning prayer service

SHAILOS — (pl.) halakhic queries

SHALOM BAYIS — peace in the home

SHAS — lit. the six orders of the Mishna; the Talmud

SHEMONEH ESREI — lit. eighteen; the central prayer in Jewish liturgy which is recited three times daily

SHEVA BRACHOS — 1. the seven benedictions recited at a wedding and in the presence of the newlyweds during the first week of their marriage; 2. the seven days after a wedding

SHIUR — Torah lecture

SHIUR KLALI — lit. general lecture; advanced lecture usually delivered by the senior ROSH YESHIVA

SHIVA — lit. seven; the seven day mourning period following a death

SHMAD — apostasy

SHMINI ATZERES — the eighth day of SUKKOS

SHTENDER — (Yid.) lectern, used in place of desks in many yeshivos

SHTIEBEL — (Yid.) small, informal, intimate room for prayer and study

SHUL — (Yid.) synagogue

SHULCHAN ARUKH — code of Jewish law compiled by Rabbi Yosef Karo

SIFREI KODESH — (pl.) holy books; see SEFER

SIMCHA — lit. joy; celebration

SIMCHAS TORAH — the holiday of the rejoicing of the Torah

SIYATTA DE'SHMAYA — Heavenly assistance

SIYUM — completion ceremony of a Talmudic tract

SUKKAH — temporary dwelling which is central requirement of the holiday of SUKKOS

SUKKOS — week-long Autumn festival during which time one dwells in a SUKKAH

TAAM — lit. taste; enjoyment

TAHARAS HAMISHPACHA — family purity

TALMID (TALMIDIM) — student

TALMID CHACHAM (TALMIDEI CHACHAMIM) — Torah scholar

TEFILLAH — prayer; prayer service

TEHILLIM — Psalms; book of Psalms

TORAH LISHMA — Torah learning purely for its own sake

TREIFA — (Yid.) lit. torn; non-kosher; unacceptable

TSURAS ADAM — image of man

TZADDIK — righteous man

VERTLACH — (Yid.) (pl.) words; a short, novel explanation of a Torah concept

VESAIN BRACHA — and give a blessing

VIDUY — confessional prayer

VORT — (Yid.) lit. word; short novel explanation

YADIN YADIN — rabbinic ordination awarded for proficiency in the section of SHULCHAN ARUKH which deals with torts

YAHRZEIT — (Yid.) anniversary of a death

YARMULKA — (Yid.) skullcap; head covering worn by religious Jewish men

YESHIVA SHEL MAALAH — lit. Heavenly assembly; place of TZADDIKIM in Heaven

YESHIVA SHEL MATAH — lit. earthly assembly; where mankind meets to study Torah

YICHUD — forbidden seclusion with the opposite sex

YIDDEN — (Yid.) Jews

YIDDISHE — (Yid.) Jewish

YINGELEH — (Yid.) little boy

YOMIM NORAIM — days of awe; ten days of penitence from Rosh Hashanah through Yom Kippur

YOM TOV — holiday

YOSEF HATZADDIK — lit. Joseph the righteous; biblical Joseph

ZMAN — yeshiva semester

ZT"L — abbreviation for "may the memory of the TZADDIK be blessed"